UNSTUCK

THE SIMPLIFIED BLUEPRINT FOR BUSY ADULTS WHO WANT TO START STRONG, STAY MOTIVATED, AND FINISH WHAT MATTERS

VALARIE V. HENRY

ISBN: 979-8-9995387-0-3

CONTENTS

Success is not the key to happiness. Happiness is the key to success. If you love what you are doing, you will be successful.

— ALBERT SCHWEITZER

INTRODUCTION

Let's be honest. If I had a dollar for every time I set a goal and watched it quietly sneak out the back door, I'd have enough money to open a Failed Goals Hall of Fame. (Admission: free with proof of a forgotten gym membership.) If you're reading this, you've had your own version of this experience. Maybe the "start running" goal turned into "buy new sneakers and watch Netflix." Or the "write that novel" plan that ended up as a detailed grocery list. Here's the thing: we all have big dreams. We all make promises to ourselves. And yet, most of us have a graveyard of half-finished projects, lost motivation, and goals still sitting on the bench, waiting for their shot.

Now, who am I to be guiding you on this journey? I'm Dr. Valarie Henry. I've worn many hats over the years—retail worker, personal trainer, sales representative, and, ultimately, educator. My twenty-plus years in education have included a variety of roles and titles, including teacher, school administrator, and central office administrator; along the way, I also earned a doctorate in Instructional Leadership. Those are just a few of the goals I have completed!

The common thread in all my roles has been working with people. I've spent my career exploring what makes people tick and how we can do better, be better, and feel better. My obsession with human behavior started as a child (youngest of six siblings), then again in college, inspired over the years by legends like Abraham Maslow. My organic leadership strengths, including connectedness, relationship building, and achievement (Gallup, 2025), fueled my mission to write books that are helpful, hopeful, and fun.

Now, let's address the elephant in the room. There are about a zillion books on goal setting out there. If I stacked them all up, I could reach the moon (or at least a sturdy second-story window). So why write another one? Most of those books do a great job of telling you to set SMART goals, make lists, and color-code your life—but they rarely dig deeper. They don't ask you to pause and look in the mirror. They don't help you figure out what's driving you or why you sometimes sabotage yourself before you even start. And they sure don't talk about what to do when your motivation packs its bags and heads to the Bahamas.

This book is different. "Unstuck" is for anyone who wants more than just a checklist. It's for you if you crave real change, not just another planner collecting dust. Yes, you'll get practical tools. You'll learn how to break down your goals, make plans that work, and finish what you start. But you'll also dig into the "why" behind your goals. Why do you want what you want? Why do you quit when things get tough? Why does chasing your dream sometimes feel like wrestling a greased pig? (Spoiler: there are real, science-backed reasons for all this!)

Understanding your "why" is more important than knowing "how" to do something—at least at the start. If your reasons for chasing a goal aren't strong, clear, and personal, even the best system will collapse when life gets messy. That's why Chapter One is all about helping you uncover your true motivations. We'll get honest; it may be a little uncomfortable and weird. But I promise: it'll be worth it.

This book isn't just built on theory and wishful thinking. I've spent years researching what works (and what doesn't) with real people. I've worked with students, teachers, parents, leaders, and teams who all wanted to change something—big or small. I've read the research, ran the workshops, conducted the interviews, and made plenty of mistakes. Their stories, struggles, and successes are baked into every chapter. So, when I say you're not alone, I mean it. You'll see yourself in these pages and pick up tips that work in the wild.

You won't just read about ideas; you'll act on them. This book is packed with interactive exercises, reflection prompts, and mini challenges. You'll be nudged (maybe even lovingly shoved) out of your comfort zone. There are spaces for your answers, doodles, and moments of "aha!" You're not just a reader—you're a participant. Please write in the margins, cross things out, and return to these pages whenever you need a boost.

Now, let's talk about the voices in your head. Maybe you're thinking, "I've tried before and failed." Or "I'm too busy. I don't have time for another project." Or even, "Goals are for other people—people who have it all together." Trust me, I've heard it all. You don't need to have superhuman discipline or a color-coded spreadsheet for every hour of your day. You must be willing to start, stumble, and keep going when things get tough. Perfection is not required. Progress is.

If you commit to this process, you'll see real change. You'll learn how to set goals that matter to you, not just to your boss, your parents, or your favorite motivational Instagram account. You'll get tools to keep going when excitement fades. You'll learn how to recover from setbacks, adjust your plan without guilt, and finish what you start. You'll move from vision to victory—one honest, unglamorous, glorious step at a time.

So, here's my invitation let's do this together. You bring your dreams, doubts, and determination. I'll get decades of research, a dash of humor, and a truckload of real talk. This isn't just another book on goals. It's your permission slip to dream bigger, start bolder, and finish stronger.

Ready? Let's get moving. Your blueprint starts now.

The key is not to prioritize what's on your schedule, but to schedule your priorities.

— STEPHEN COVEY

1

LAYING THE GROUNDWORK— FROM OVERWHELM TO CLARITY

A popular meme sums up modern mental chaos: "My brain is like a browser with 47 tabs open. Four are frozen. I don't know where the music is coming from." If juggling endless ambitions, deadlines, and random tasks gives you anxiety, you're not alone. Setting goals sounds simple, but sorting through the mess of "shoulds," "could," and "maybe-somedays" in your head is daunting—sometimes, just picking a starting point feels impossible. Society encourages us to pursue countless goals, suggesting it's a path to greatness. Progress starts when you clear the clutter and focus on what truly deserves your attention.

As a teacher, I watched students frantically balance schoolwork, sports, jobs, and family expectations. As an administrator, I met educators burning out as they attempted to excel everywhere. I've been there myself, with a to-do list ranging from academic publishing to half-marathons, French lessons, and sourdough baking (my starters still hold a grudge). Wanting to "do it all" is common, but it's not a strategy—it only leads to mediocrity and frustration. The real break-through happens when you accept that not every task deserves your energy.

THE "GOAL CLARITY AUDIT"—ZEROING IN ON WHAT MATTERS

Here's where you trade chaos for clarity. The "Goal Clarity Audit" is spring cleaning for your ambitions. It helps you sort through mental clutter and uncover which goals are truly yours—not just the loudest or most urgent. All you need is a notebook, an open mind, and maybe a snack for morale.

Start with a brain dump: write down every goal, wish, pressure, and stray idea in your head. There is no need to judge or filter—list every-thing, realistic or not. Your list may be huge or humble. For instance, Jamie listed "get promoted at work," "run three times a week," "fix things with my brother," "take a pottery class," and "stop doom-scrolling before bed." Yours may be messier or more straightforward.

Now, sort your goals. For each, ask yourself: Did I choose this out of excitement, habit, or obligation? Do I carry it out of genuine desire or just guilt? Use this checklist and scoring system:

- Does this excite me (2), feel neutral (1), or stress me out (0)?
- Is this urgent (2), important but not urgent (1), or neither (0)?
- Does this fit my values (2), kind of fit (1), or clash (0)? Add up each goal's score—higher totals mean higher priority.

Goal Clarity Audit Worksheet

1. List all current goals, wishes, and obligations.
2. For each, answer:
   - Does it excite/inspire or stress you?
   - Is it urgent, important, or just loud?
   - Does it align with your values?
3. Score: Excitement (0-2), Urgency (0-2), Value Fit (0-2).
4. Total the scores.
5. Circle your 1-2 highest scorers.

Review your list. Most people find that half their goals have low scores—they're more of a burden than help. Jamie's eight goals shrank to two that truly excited her: reconnecting with her brother and prepping for a work presentation that could lead to promotion. She let the others go, lightening her mental load and easing her stress.

For each remaining goal, ask: Does working on this energize or drain me? Sometimes urgency is just mental noise—your email backlog rarely outranks your long-term dreams. Doubting the "urgent" stuff helps you focus on what moves you forward.

This audit is honest. You see all your ambitions immediately, without pressure to do everything now. You pick one or two priority goals and give yourself permission to focus. You can revisit the rest later. Doing less—and doing it better—brings instant relief and makes your next steps clearer.

Grab your pen, empty your mental filing cabinet, and figure out what truly matters to you—not what's loudest, not what's trendy, but what genuinely excites and suits your life right now.

DITCHING THE NOISE—FILTERING OUT BORROWED AND DISTRACTING GOALS

Everywhere you turn, someone tells you what you "should" want—Instagram influencers with marathon medals, LinkedIn announcements about promotions, even Aunt Linda bragging about learning Mandarin at 50. No wonder your ambitions get tangled up in all this noise. The truth? Not every goal in your mind is yours. Some are borrowed from social media, family, or culture, disguised as "self-improvement" but draining and exhausting. Chasing someone else's dream or following a checklist that isn't yours leads to burnout, like running in shoes that don't fit. Consider joining a marathon because your friends did, even though you hate running and dislike the gym. Or maybe you're climbing the corporate ladder simply because it's expected, despite dreading every meeting.

Borrowed ambitions are subtle. They whisper, "Everyone else is doing it—don't get left behind." Before long, you're deep into a pursuit that leaves you bored, frazzled, or miserable. You lose motivation and blame your willpower when the real issue is you were aiming for someone else's finish line all along. So, how do you find your own signal amid the noise? Start by pausing to notice the voices guiding your choices. Imagine reaching a goal—whose voice do you hear cheering or criticizing you? A parent, a trend, or your own genuine excitement? Grab a notebook and reflect: Write down a goal you feel pressured to pursue, then ask yourself, "Whose approval am I really seeking?" If it's not your own, mentally flag that goal.

Here's a checklist to trace the roots of your ambitions:

- Does this goal excite me, or does it just stress me out?
- If nobody knew, would I still want to do it?
- Who first put this idea in my mind?
- Would letting this go feel like relief or regret?
- Is this tied to my core values or just outside expectations?

Use these questions to review your goal list with the "Me or Not Me" test. If pursuing it fills you with dread or quitting brings only relief, it probably isn't yours. Sometimes, saying "no" is the surest way to happiness and focus.

Worried you'll disappoint others or feel like a failure by letting go? The truth is that dropping borrowed ambitions clears space for what matters to you. If guilt crops up, try this: "I'm letting go of this goal because it belongs to someone else's story—not mine. I respect why it matters to them, but I have different priorities." Use this whenever you need to reclaim your energy.

A coworkers once told me she trained for months for a triathlon to keep up with friends who said it would be "life changing." Each workout felt like punishment, and she counted down to when she could quit without looking flaky. She eventually stopped and focused on writing her novel instead. Her words: "I felt lighter instantly. My energy came back. I realized the only person who needed to be proud of my goals was me."

It's easy to be swept up by others' excitement, especially now when sharing achievements is just a click away. But chasing borrowed dreams is like wearing someone else's glasses—everything's blurry, and soon you get a headache. Your most explicit focus comes from dropping goals that aren't really yours.

Here's a quick self-audit:

Checklist: Is This My Goal or Someone Else's?

- I feel energized thinking about this goal (yes/no)
- My motivation is internal (yes/no)
- Letting go would bring relief (yes/no)
- It fits my values (yes/no)
- I'd pursue it even if nobody noticed (yes/no)

More "no" answers than "yes"? It might be time to let go of that ambition—for now, at least. This isn't selfish, it's wise. Clearing out borrowed goals makes space for authentic satisfaction and progress. When you say yes only to what truly matters, your energy and results will surprise you.

IDENTIFYING YOUR "WHY"—ROOTING AMBITIONS IN TRUE MOTIVATION

You've whittled your goals down to the ones that matter, and now you're left staring at them, wondering why they sometimes feel as slippery as a bar of soap in a public shower. Here's the twist: unless you know the real reason, you care about a goal, motivation will evaporate faster than your enthusiasm for salad on pizza night. Surface-level reasons—like "because I should" or "because everyone else is doing it"—crumble under pressure. To stick with something when Netflix, snacks, and the snooze button all start calling your name, you need a reason that makes your pulse quicken or at least makes you say, "Yes, that's it. That's why I'm getting off the couch."

I love using the "5 Whys" exercise for this. It's simple: take your goal and ask yourself "Why?" five times, each answer digging deeper into your motivation. For example, say your initial goal is, "I want a raise." First, why: Why do you want a raise? "Because I want more money." Second why: Why do you want more money? "So, I can pay off my debts." Third, why: Why is that important? "Because I'm tired of worrying about bills." Fourth, why: Why does that matter? "Because I want to feel secure and independent." Fifth, why: Why is independence so important to you? "Because I had to rely on others when I was younger, which made me feel powerless." Suddenly, getting a raise isn't just about dollars; it's about reclaiming control over your life. The deeper you go, the more personal—and powerful—your motivation becomes.

Let's try another one. You may be targeting weight loss. First, why: Why do you want to lose 10 pounds? "To look better." Second: Why do you care about looking better? "Because I want to feel confident in my clothes." Third: Why is confidence necessary? "Because I want to be energetic and playful with my kids." Fourth: Why do you crave that energy? "Because I remember how happy they look when I join their games." Fifth: Why does that happiness matter? "Because those moments make me feel connected and alive." The quest isn't about a number on the scale; it's about capturing those bursts of joy and connection with your children.

The emotional connection to your goal is your rocket fuel. If your reason doesn't spark emotion—something you can feel in your body or that makes you nod and think, "Yes, that's exactly it"—motivation will run dry halfway through. Use this quick checklist to test your "why": Does thinking about this reason make me feel something— excitement, relief, hope, pride? If yes, chances are you've struck gold. If not, dig again.

Why Statement Template

Here's a template to craft your own why statement for each goal:

"I want to [goal] because [deeper reason]. Achieving this will help me [personal impact]."

For instance:

"I want to write my book because sharing my story matters. Achieving this will help me inspire others and prove to myself that my voice is important."

Write your why statement in a notebook, sticky note in your bathroom mirror, or on your phone's lock screen. Visual reminders keep your motivation front and center.

Now, let's make it real with a visualization exercise. Take a few moments. Close your eyes. Picture yourself reaching your goal—feel it as if it's happening right now. Imagine walking into work after getting that raise. What do you see? Is your boss shaking your hand? Is your inbox full of congratulations? Notice what emotions bubble up. Pride? Relief? Security? Or see yourself playing outside with your kids, light on your feet, laughter echoing around you. How does your body feel? What expression is on your face?

Visualization isn't fluff—it helps solidify your "why" by connecting thought with feeling (A psychologist explains the power of 'vision boarding' for success, 2024). The more precise the emotional picture, the more anchored your commitment becomes.

Our brains are wired for stories and emotions. When you root your goals in honest, personal motivation and tie them to vivid mental images, they become far more than tasks on a list—they turn into promises to yourself that matter too much to abandon when things get tough. Write down at least one detailed why statement and practice picturing what success feels like; this becomes the foundation you'll return to whenever distraction or doubt threatens to pull you off track.

PAIN POINT MAPPING—TURNING STRUGGLES INTO STARTING POINTS

Let's be real: chasing goals is rarely smooth. Most people have unfinished projects, abandoned hobbies, and wasted gym memberships. The first step to making real progress is acknowledging what's holding you back—not dwelling on failures but using your struggles as signposts for what needs attention. Grab a notebook or notes app— you're about to get honest. Think about your most stubborn goals: what consistently trips you up? Maybe you start strong but lose motivation quickly or pledge to focus, only to get scattered as soon as life gets busy.

Try this: "What's frustrated me most about my goals?" Write down anything that comes up—no filters, no shame. For many, the main issue is a loss of momentum after the initial excitement fades. Others get overwhelmed by juggling too many priorities, abandoning each halfway through. Common pitfalls include procrastinating until the last minute, negative self-talk ("I'll never finish this anyway"), or letting minor setbacks become reasons to quit.

Here's the key: mapping these pain points to concrete starting steps turns obstacles into guides. Instead of seeing them as proof you're "bad at goals," treat them like arrows pointing to where you need to start. Consider this:

Pain Point First Actionable Step

Losing motivation quickly -- Schedule a weekly check-in and reward

Too many priorities -- Choose ONE goal to prioritize this month

Burnout after two weeks -- Build in mini-breaks and energy rituals

Procrastination -- Set micro-deadlines with reminders

Negative self-talk -- Write a daily "done" list, not just a "to-do."

For example, if you always burn out after two weeks, don't just try harder—make your first move about managing energy. Maybe that means a daily walk or blocking off time for breaks. If you struggle with juggling too many projects, pick just one to focus on for 30 days.

I once worked with someone who always burned out halfway through big projects—at work and in her personal life. She thought she lacked discipline, but mapping her pain points revealed she never scheduled recovery. Her first step became an "energy audit" and planning mini breaks before starting. She made it past the two-week slump for the first time in years.

Worksheet: My Top 3 Triggers and My First Responses

Get specific about what knocks you off track and what you'll do in response.

1. **Trigger:** What situation or feeling derails your progress?
2. **First Response:** What's one thing you'll do when this happens?
3. **Trigger:**
4. **First Response:**
5. **Trigger:**
6. **First Response:**

Examples:

1. **Trigger:** Feeling wiped out after work and losing motivation
2. **First Response:** Listen to upbeat music for 10 minutes before starting a task
3. **Trigger:** Overwhelmed by too much to do
4. **First Response:** Tackle just one urgent task and ignore the rest until it's done
5. **Trigger:** Falling into negative self-talk after missing a day
6. **First Response:** Write down at least one thing accomplished, however small

When you chart your common pitfalls this way, old patterns lose some power. Each frustration becomes a clue—if losing momentum is your main hurdle, your first step could be regular check-ins and celebrating small wins. If procrastination trips you up, break tasks into small pieces that are hard to put off.

Pain points are not proof you aren't capable; they're signals guiding you toward missing skills or supports. If burnout is constant, recovery must come first, not last. When you map your struggles to actionable starting steps, you create a plan tailored to your life—not just another generic list. Please fill out the worksheet honestly and keep it handy. These notes become your troubleshooting guide for when things get tough.

MAKING PEACE WITH THE BLANK SLATE—OVERCOMING THE FEAR TO BEGIN

Nothing strikes fear into the heart quite like a fresh start. You stare at that empty page, untouched planner, or blinking cursor and suddenly remember every failed attempt, every abandoned project, and every New Year's resolution that fizzled before Valentine's Day. It's almost comical how a simple blank notebook can make a grown adult sweat like they're facing a pop quiz they didn't study for. That first step feels loaded with pressure. "What if I mess up?" "What if I start and can't finish?" "What if I'm not cut out for this at all?" These thoughts play on a loop, paralyzing even the most ambitious among us.

Let me tell you about someone we'll call "The Perfectionist." She had a new project—organizing a community art show. She spent weeks researching, planning, and color-coding her spreadsheet. She froze when it came time to send out invites and book the venue. The pressure to get every detail right initially was so intense that she abandoned the whole idea rather than risk a messy start. That's the perfectionist freeze: the idea that you shouldn't launch unless you launch perfectly. It's as if we believe our first step must look like the highlight reel we see on social media, but real life is rarely that polished.

Here's something I wish I could shout from a rooftop: messy beginnings are not just normal but productive. In fact, science and experience both suggest that getting started, even when you feel unprepared, is far more valuable than waiting for the "perfect" moment (The Psychology Group, n.d.). I call it the "launch ugly" philosophy. Imagine building a sandcastle: the first scoop of sand is always lumpy, uneven, and never Instagram-worthy. But you can't create anything beautiful until you get your hands dirty. Starting awkwardly is infinitely better than not starting at all. You can always revise, tweak, or pivot later but can't improve what doesn't exist.

If fear of failure plays on your nerves like an out-of-tune piano, try shifting your mindset from "this must succeed" to "this is only an experiment." Treat your first week as a trial run—a low-stakes rehearsal rather than a life-or-death performance. Give yourself permission to tinker, stumble, or even backtrack without judgment. Picture your first attempts as sketches, not final drafts. If you're learning guitar, allow yourself to strum off-key without embarrassment. If you're starting a side hustle, let your first post or product be clumsy. The key is to treat mistakes as data, not proof you're doomed.

Research backs up this experimental approach. Studies show that when people view their initial efforts as learning opportunities instead of final judgments, their anxiety drops, and their creativity rises (The Psychology Group, n.d.). Starting becomes less about demonstrating worth and more about gathering information—what works for you, what doesn't, and how you might adjust next time. When framed as an experiment, setbacks become feedback rather than dead ends.

Now for your "first action" challenge—the antidote to inertia. Pick one minuscule step related to your goal and do it today. Not tomorrow, not next week—today. Want to start writing? Open a document and type the date at the top. Dream of running? Put sneakers by the door or text a friend to meet for a walk. Thinking about learning Spanish? Download an app or write "Hola" on a sticky note and slap it on your fridge. These are tiny moves but shatter the illusion that action requires epic readiness.

If you crave accountability (and let's face it, most of us do), send yourself a calendar invite or text someone close: "I'm starting my project today—hold me to it!" Buy a fresh notebook or set up a free account in one of those fancy goal-tracking apps (ClickUp, 2025). The goal here isn't grandeur; it's momentum. Momentum is like riding a bike—the most challenging part is that first awkward pedal, but once you're moving, balance comes easier, and confidence grows with every wobble.

Perfection isn't invited to this party. Progress is. Every expert began as a beginner willing to look silly for a while. Your blank slate is not an accusation—it's an invitation. Let your first move be ugly, uncoordinated, or even laughable if it has to be. Just make it real. Take that step today and watch what happens when possibility replaces paralysis.

Success is liking yourself, liking what you do, and liking how you do it.

— MAYA ANGELOU

2

VISION CRAFTING— DESIGNING YOUR PERSONAL DEFINITION OF SUCCESS

THE VISION BOARDING WORKSHOP—BRINGING DREAMS INTO FOCUS

C an you instantly recall the look of your favorite pizza but struggle to envision your most important goal? That's because our minds work in images, not bullet points. Vision boards aren't just a Pinterest trend—they help you concentrate your energy on what truly matters. If you feel like you're constantly pursuing someone else's definition of success or your dreams are buried under daily tasks, it's time to get visual and craft your version of the good life.

You can go classic with scissors, glue, and magazines or digital with tools like Canva, Pinterest, or a simple slide deck. Gather magazines if you like working with your hands or open a Pinterest board if you prefer digital inspiration. The first step is to collect images, words, and colors that grab your attention and feel like "you." Don't edit or judge. Whether it's a mountain sunrise, a quirky doodle, a cozy library, or "courage" in bold letters, notice what draws you in—often, your subconscious knows what you want before you consciously recognize it.

Once you have your collection, arrange your images into a collage. If you're using Canva, drag them around until it feels right. Build a "My Next Chapter" board on Pinterest and pin freely. There's no need for perfection—focus on what resonates, not on making art. Personalize your board with doodles, favorite quotes, ticket stubs, or colors that make you smile.

Science supports this visual process. Studies show that picturing an experience—like nailing a big presentation or crossing a marathon finish line—activates motivation and reward centers in your brain, almost as if you're experiencing it for real (Travers, 2024). Regularly looking at your vision board strengthens these neural pathways, making your envisioned success feel familiar and achievable. Visualization also activates the brain's Reticular Activating System (RAS), which filters distractions and flags anything connected to your goals as necessary.

Don't only focus on clear-cut goals like "own a home" or "get promoted." The best vision boards include feelings, settings, and values. Ask yourself: What does an ideal day feel like? Who's with you? Is the mood calm, energetic, and creative? If stress reduction is key, include tranquil landscapes. If relationships matter, add images of people connecting. If you're after adventure, pick bold activities or wild places that reflect your desired energy and life.

If creating a collage feels overwhelming, try different formats. Consider a vision mind map: Put "Future Me" in the center, and branch out with words or small sketches for your priorities, values, and feelings. This works well if you like connecting ideas visually without magazine clippings. Prefer a sequence? Try storyboarding: Sketch a series of "scenes" in boxes—waking up energized, working on a cool project, cooking with friends. Each frame gives another glimpse of your personal success.

Quick Interactive Exercise: Your First Vision Board Sprint

Set a 15-minute timer. Find five images (in print or online) that excite you about any area of life—career, health, relationships, fun. Arrange them in front of you. Write down three words for each image describing how it makes you feel. Step back—what themes emerge? Where do you see patterns in what you want more of? Let this mini board be a starting point; add to it as your vision expands.

Vision boards aren't about predicting the future—they help clarify what matters, aligning your brain and heart. No matter your style—tactile or tech-savvy—visualizing where you want to go primes your mind for action and unlocks clarity and creativity that lists alone can't provide.

VISUALIZATION DEEP DIVE—SEEING YOUR FUTURE SELF IN ACTION

Imagine waking up tomorrow and living the life you've always wanted—no, really picture it, down to the smallest detail. Before you roll your eyes and say, "Sure, Dr. Henry, let me just manifest myself on a private jet," hear me out. This isn't about wishful thinking or chanting at your vision board. This is about structured visualization—a mental exercise that helps you build a future that feels so real that your brain starts treating it as a blueprint rather than a fairy tale.

Start by closing your eyes and breathing deeply a few times. Now, let's mentally walk through a successful day in your future life. Where does it begin? Maybe you open your eyes to sunlight streaming through a window in a place that truly feels like home—an apartment with plants everywhere, a cabin in the woods, or just a bedroom that finally stays clean for over three days. What does the air smell like in this space? Crisp, maybe with a hint of coffee or fresh-cut grass? Listen: are birds singing? Is there quiet, or do you hear the gentle buzz of city life outside?

You slide out of bed—what do you feel beneath your feet? A soft rug, cool tiles, the warmth of a pet greeting you? Make breakfast and tune into those sensory details: the sizzle of eggs, the aroma of cinnamon toast, and the taste of perfectly brewed coffee. As you move through this day, notice who is with you. Are there kids' giggles in the background, a roommate humming along to music, or maybe it's just peaceful solitude? What clothes do you reach for? How do they feel against your skin—comfortable, empowering, perhaps even a little fancy for no reason?

Picture yourself heading into your work or creative space. What do you see on the walls—artwork, sticky notes with ideas, sunlight pouring over your laptop? Hear the sounds around you: typing keys, soft music, maybe even the click-clack of your favorite shoes. Pay attention to how you feel as you start working on something meaningful—a big project, creative challenge, or helping someone. Energized? Calm? Focused and proud? Let yourself notice emotional shifts as you move through this imagined day: confidence rising during a meeting, joy when you help someone, satisfaction after a workout, or when you finish a task that matters.

Lunch with friends or family might show up next in this mental movie. Taste the food. Feel the laughter bubbling up unexpectedly. Smell fresh salad greens or spicy noodles. The afternoon might bring more accomplishments—maybe you solve a tricky problem or finally finish something nagging at you forever. You look up and realize how present and engaged you feel.

Evening arrives: what does relaxation look like for you? Is it reading by the window, walking as the sun sets, or sharing a meal with people who lift you up? As you wind down, reflect on the day. What are you most grateful for? What emotions linger as you crawl into bed—peace, pride, excitement for tomorrow? Let all five senses fill in this world: the softness of blankets, the gentle glow of bedside lights, even the faint scent of lavender from your pillow spray.

While doing this exercise, capture any unexpected details or feelings. Maybe you realized how much natural light matters or that sharing food with others brings you joy. The sound of laughter tells you connection is a core value. Sometimes, the smallest moments—like putting on running shoes or hearing your favorite playlist—hold surprising weight.

Worksheet: Unexpected Elements from My Visualization

Take a few minutes after your mental walk-through to jot down any surprising observations or emotions. Did something appear that you didn't expect—a dog running circles around your feet or a quiet moment alone that felt deeply satisfying? Write these down in a journal or notes app. These hidden treasures are clues for building goals that go beyond surface-level achievements.

Here's the secret sauce: repeat this visualization ritual often—daily, if possible, weekly at minimum. The more regularly you mentally "live" as your future self, the more familiar and believable it becomes. Over time, your brain starts to accept this identity shift; suddenly, action toward these goals feels natural instead of forced. Ritual repetition isn't about superstition but building deep neural grooves that doubt has trouble crawling out of. You're not just dreaming; you're training your mind to see yourself as someone who achieves what matters most.

THE "SUCCESS SNAPSHOT"—CRAFTING A TANGIBLE, INSPIRING ENDGAME

Think about the one photo you'd frame if you finally reached your biggest goal. It's not a stock photo of a trophy but something genuinely yours. Picture what's happening at that moment. Are you grinning ear-to-ear with a college diploma in hand, or maybe standing at the front of a packed auditorium, applause washing over you after a presentation you once thought impossible? This snapshot isn't just for show. It's a pin on your mental map, a destination you can return to when your motivation threatens to bail. I often ask myself, "What's the one scene that would make all the hard work worth it?" For some, it's hugging a loved one after finishing a marathon, sweat, and pride mixing equally. For others, watching a child's face light up as you walk through the door proves that your commitment to work-life balance is paying off. Maybe it's even simpler: sitting at your favorite café, first copy of your book in hand, sunlight slanting through the window.

Specificity is key here. Vague ideas like "be successful," "get in shape," or "be happy" won't cut it. You need detail so sharp it almost pricks your fingers. If your snapshot is running a race, don't just see the finish line—hear your shoes slap the pavement, feel your heart hammering, taste the salt on your lips, and spot your best friend jumping up and down in the crowd. If you aim for career success, can you describe when your mentor shakes your hand and says, "You did it"? What does their face look like? Does relief flood your body? Are your palms still sweating? The more senses you engage, the more real this scene becomes in your mind. Ask yourself these questions: Can I picture this? Do I feel something when I imagine it? Could I describe it to someone else without them squinting in confusion?

This isn't just about painting pretty pictures for yourself. Your snapshot is a tool for resilience in real life. This vivid image becomes a filter when you're knee-deep in setbacks, tired from tackling endless tasks, or stuck between two tough decisions. Should you say "yes" to that extra project? Does it bring you closer to your snapshot or drag you away? When you feel tempted to quit after a rough day, pull out that mental polaroid. Remember why you started and what victory will look and feel like—not just in theory but in living color.

Decision fatigue tends to sneak up on us, especially when our goals start feeling distant or abstract. This is when the snapshot steps up as your anchor. Stuck between an easy out and a move that's scary but necessary? Revisit your framed moment: Does the easy path match what's in the picture, or is discomfort where growth happens? In challenging moments, your snapshot isn't just inspiration—it's decision-making ammo.

Boiling down this vibrant scene into one or two sentences can be powerful. A clear summary glues the image and gives you a mantra for tough days. I use a template: "I will know I've succeeded when..." and then fill in the sensory details and emotions that matter most. For instance: "I will know I've succeeded when standing under the stage lights, heart racing as I close my speech and see my family clapping in the front row." Or maybe: "I'll know I've made it when I unlock my shop door in the morning and smell fresh bread baking—freedom and pride mixed in the air." Don't be afraid to get personal or even a little weird; this is your finish line, not anyone else's.

If you want to go further, create a checklist: Can I see this snapshot clearly? Does imagining it stir up emotion—excitement, pride, gratitude, relief? Can I describe at least three details about what's happening? If you answer yes all around, you're on the right path. If not, keep digging until it gets real enough to matter.

Think of this scene as your lighthouse and life raft—guiding you forward and keeping you afloat through rough waters. When the temptation to quit hits or self-doubt creeps in, return to this moment. No matter how scattered things get or how often life tries to knock you off course, this snapshot grounds you in what matters most. Write it down somewhere visible—a sticky notes on your mirror, a note on your phone, or even a doodle on your desk blotter. When things get tough—and they will—this scene reminds you why every step forward counts.

BUILDING YOUR "WINS WALL"—CELEBRATING MICRO-SUCCESSES FROM DAY ONE

A significant flaw in how most people chase big goals is spending so much time dreaming about the finish line that we forget to celebrate the actual trek. That's like hiking a mountain, ignoring every breath-taking view, and only cheering when you finally reach the summit—assuming you don't get lost somewhere around base camp. What if you could build a trail of mini trophies right from the start? That's where your "Wins Wall" comes in. This isn't some corny motivational poster situation. It's a real, tangible, or digital space dedicated to recording every forward step—no matter how tiny, trivial, or "not worth mentioning" it seems at the time.

Imagine your bedroom door covered with neon sticky notes, each shouting out a different win: "Sent that awkward email," "Walked ten minutes after work," or "Didn't eat the entire pizza." Or you're more of a tech enthusiast, so you set up a private Slack channel for yourself (or your accountability group) and drop in daily updates with the best emoji reactions you can find. If you love organization, a Notion database or Google Doc can work wonders—log each win with date stamps and even attach photos for extra flair. The format doesn't matter; finding what feels fun or satisfying is key. Some people even use their phone's photo album, snapping pictures of little achievements—a finished to-do list, a clean workspace, a healthy lunch. Over time, those images become a flipbook of progress.

Why bother with this? Here's the not-so-secret sauce: your brain craves recognition more than you realize. When you celebrate small wins, you train your mind to seek more opportunities for progress. This isn't just motivational fluff; it's neuroscience. Every time you acknowledge an achievement—however minor—your brain releases dopamine, which boosts motivation and attention (Sinek, n.d.). It's like giving your internal cheerleader a megaphone. The more often you spot and savor these micro-victories, the more likely you are to keep moving forward when things get tough. Researchers have found that those who regularly record their progress are significantly more likely to stick with long-term goals than those who only focus on the result. Why? Tracking small wins lights up those reward pathways that try feel worth it.

You don't need to wait for "big moments" to start building your Wins Wall. In fact, starting on day one is the best hack I know for beating discouragement before it even shows up. The trick is to lower the bar for what counts as a win—if you got out of bed and put on gym shoes (note: I didn't say you worked out), that's a square on the wall. Sent an email you've been avoiding for three days? Another win. Chose water over soda just once? That's wall-worthy. Over time, these micro-rewards add up like compound interest, creating a sense of momentum that's hard to ignore.

Getting creative with your Wins Wall design can make the habit even stickier. For tactile folks, a cork board with colorful push pins or ribbons can turn your workspace into a gallery of progress. List lovers might opt for a whiteboard grid they can fill in with dry-erase markers—there's something satisfying about erasing and rewriting those wins each week. If you're always on the go, try a "Win's" folder in your phone's notes app or a rolling photo album of evidence (screenshots count!). For group accountability, set up a shared Google Doc or Slack thread where everyone posts at least one win per week—public recognition gives a double shot of dopamine.

Don't let your Wins Wall become wallpaper. Schedule regular check-ins to review and celebrate what's there. Every other Friday or the last Sunday of each month, take ten minutes to scan your board, scroll through your album, or read your list aloud (bonus points if you do it out loud and embarrass your pet). If you have an accountability partner or mastermind group, make this ritual social—trade wins with each other and offer virtual high-fives or memes as rewards. These review sessions aren't about bragging but wiring your brain for consistency and confidence.

You'll likely notice patterns: some weeks will overflow with colorful notes or digital badges, while others may feel light. That's normal. The point is not perfection but persistence—proving to yourself that progress is always happening, even when it feels slow. Over time, this habit builds a visual record of grit and growth—a Wins Wall that cheers you on long after motivation does its usual disappearing act.

PERSONALIZING YOUR VICTORY—DEFINING WHAT WINNING LOOKS LIKE FOR YOU

Many people chase "success," only to find they've climbed someone else's ladder—and end up feeling underwhelmed when the fireworks never come. This disconnect often happens when you let society define what victory means. It's like following the crowd's order at a restaurant, only to realize you don't even like what's on your plate. The world offers constant suggestions—money, status, likes, or flashy cars—but they're meaningless if these wins don't make you proud when no one's watching.

Take a moment to ask yourself: What would still feel like a win if no one ever noticed or celebrated your achievements? It isn't about promotion but the joy of waking up without dread, not a bigger house, and the luxury of having time to draw or play music after dinner. There's real strength in quietly choosing what brings you pride, even if your version of victory looks very different from everyone else's.

If you're unsure how to define success, try exploring non-traditional metrics—joy, freedom, impact, and growth. These are just as valuable as money or prestige. Some people use "peace of mind," measuring progress by how well they sleep instead of their income. Others value "creative fulfillment," feeling accomplished when they finish a painting or write a journal page. Some measure success through "impact on others"—mentoring, volunteering, or simply being a good friend. The essential step is to find metrics that make you feel alive and genuinely satisfied, not just occupied.

Here's a simple prompt: finish this sentence—"I would feel victorious if..." Let your answer be personal and honest, no matter how unconventional. Maybe it's "spending quiet mornings reading" or "knowing my little brother trusts me." Your victories don't have to fit on a spreadsheet; often, the most rewarding wins are the ones only you notice.

To solidify this mindset, try creating a brief "victory manifesto." This isn't about creating an impressive statement for others but expressing your most accurate vision of success. It can be as simple as: "My victory is building a life where I laugh every day and support the people I care about," or "Success means having the flexibility to work anywhere while spending time with family." One person shared: "For me, victory is finishing my degree despite setbacks. I don't have to be top of the class; crossing the finish line is a win." Another wrote: "Success is measured by how many young women I've helped believe in themselves." The purpose is to identify what truly motivates you.

Remember, your definition of winning can—and should—evolve. Five years ago, you might have prioritized climbing the corporate ladder; now, you might value balance instead. That's completely normal. Life changes, and so do our dreams. Consider scheduling an annual check-in with yourself—a personal review to revisit your victory manifesto. Ask: Does this still fit? Has anything shifted? If so, update your definition without guilt or hesitation. The aim is to honor who you are now, not cling to outdated dreams.

Victory is profoundly personal and ever-changing; it grows as you do. The more honest you are about what matters most, the easier it is to block out the external noise and focus on what counts for you—not your boss, parents, or strangers online. When you're transparent about your true victories, every small step feels more meaningful, even if no one else notices.

With a vision firmly rooted in your values, you're ready for the next challenge: building resilience so setbacks don't knock you off course. Old habits and doubts can challenge even the clearest idea of victory. Next up: resetting your mindset and moving forward, even when life gets tough.

Your beliefs become your thoughts,

Your thoughts become your words,

Your words become your actions,

Your actions become your habits,

Your habits become your values,

Your values become your destiny.

— MAHATMA GANDHI

3

MINDSET MASTERY— REWIRING BELIEFS FOR SUSTAINABLE PROGRESS

UNMASKING LIMITING BELIEFS—SPOTTING HIDDEN ROADBLOCKS

Imagine standing at the edge of a swimming pool, ready to leap toward your goal, but something invisible always pulls you back. That's a limiting belief—an internal thought that insists you can't, shouldn't, or won't succeed before you even start. Limiting beliefs act as hidden "Do Not Enter" signs in your mind, sounding convincing: "I'm not disciplined," "I always quit," or "People like me don't make it."

These aren't facts—just stories repeated so often they start to feel like the truth. Yet, they quietly undermine progress, sapping motivation and making efforts feel like slogging through mud.

Limiting beliefs rarely shout; they whisper through daily self-talk, especially when you're tired or things get messy. You know you've encountered one if you feel a sudden invisible wall at the prospect of acting or a sinking feeling at trying something new. Sometimes, your mind replays old failures like a playlist of doubts. To spot these beliefs, tune in to your inner monologue whenever you set a goal or face a challenge. If you hear thoughts like "I never stick with this," "I'm not creative enough," or "It's too late for me," you've met a limiting belief.

To uncover your hidden roadblocks, try guided self-inquiry. Write down a goal that excites and scares you a bit. Ask, "What thoughts stop me from starting?" Record every thought, no matter how silly or harsh. Next, examine each one and ask, "Whose voice is this? Where did I first hear it?" Often, you'll realize these ideas stem from teachers, bosses, family, or broader social expectations—not your own reasoning.

Dig deeper by asking: "What would I attempt if I knew I couldn't fail?" This question helps bypass fear and reveals your true desires. If your answer is very different from what you pursue now, limiting beliefs are likely influencing you. Another helpful question: "What do I believe about myself that stops me from trying?" Write freely—the first answer may only scratch the surface.

You're not alone if you uncover many limiting beliefs. Here's a sample of common ones: "I don't have enough time," "I'm too old to change careers," "My family never did this," "I'm always distracted," "If I fail, everyone will notice." These often disguise deeper worries about worth and belonging. The key is to notice negative self-talk in real time, especially during setbacks. If you think, "I'll never finish this— why bother?" jot it down. Writing it out gives you valuable information.

Interactive Exercise: The Belief Log

Keep a belief log for one week. Each time a negative thought about your goals or abilities appears, write it down along with what caused it. Example:

- Monday 7:30 AM: Alarm—"I'm not a morning person."
- Wednesday 4 PM: Negative feedback—"Maybe I'm not leadership material."
- Friday 8 PM: Skipped workout—"I always quit halfway."

At the end of the week, review your entries for patterns. Do criticism or new challenges trigger more limiting beliefs? Are specific thoughts recurring like a personal theme song? This log isn't for self-criticism, just for gathering awareness. The more you track these patterns, the easier it becomes to question their truth.

Limiting beliefs grow stronger in the shadows. By shining a light on them through reflection and tracking, you see them as suggestions, not facts. Power comes not from denial but from noticing these beliefs and deciding if they deserve to stay. Next time a self-doubt arises, reach for your belief log and ask: Is this true? Or is it just an outdated story ready to be let go?

MINDSET SHIFT SCRIPTS—REPLACING DOUBT WITH ACTION

Words shape how we think. The phrases you say to yourself—out loud or in your head—can subtly influence your brain's response to challenges. This is more than motivational fluff; research shows that language can direct your brain to seek specific outcomes. If you repeatedly tell yourself, "I always mess this up," your mind starts looking for proof. But if you reframe it to, "I've struggled before, but I'm learning," your brain searches for growth opportunities. But language is the steering wheel of your mindset.

This is the power behind mindset shift scripts—short, purposeful statements interrupting limiting thoughts and nudging your mind toward progress. The point isn't to fake confidence or chant empty mantras like "I am unstoppable!" as chaos unfolds. Instead, the goal is to use believable, gently optimistic language that feels true and actionable. Coaches and therapists recommend these scripts because they help you rehearse new mental habits until they become instinctive.

Let's focus on practical examples. If you usually think, "I can't do this," try, "I can start by breaking this into small steps." Replace "I'm not good at this" with "I'm not good at this yet." That one word—"yet"—sets the stage for future progress. Here are scripts to try:

- Instead of "I never get it right," say, "I'm figuring out what works for me."
- Replace "This always goes wrong" with "Every time I try, I learn something new."
- Swap "Everyone else is better at this" for "I'm on my own path and pace."
- Rather than "What if I fail?" use, "What can I learn if it doesn't go perfectly?" Experiment by rewriting your own doubts using these templates. It may initially feel strange, but repetition helps the new scripts feel natural.

Practice using mindset scripts, especially in challenging moments: before a tough call, staring at a blank screen, or after critical feedback. Notice your old thoughts ("Here we go again—I'm going to embarrass myself") and consciously replace them with something more supportive ("I might be nervous, but I've handled tough stuff before"). Please write down your favorite scripts on sticky notes, keep them in your planner, or save them as phone reminders to keep them top of mind.

For scripts to work, they must be believable. If "I am totally confident" feels false, go with "I'm working on feeling more confident" or "I'm learning to trust myself in new situations." Keep it real—you aren't trying to force yourself into believing fantasy, just stretching what you can accept. Tailor the tone to suit you. If you're usually sarcastic, let some humor in: "Sure, I'm nervous—but hey, at least I showed up."

When a script feels awkward or artificial, get more specific or add action: Instead of, "I don't know how to do this," try, "I don't know this —yet—but I can watch one tutorial today." Humor helps, too: "If I flop, at least I'll have a great story." Record your favorite scripts as voice notes or type them into your phone for quick reminders during stressful times. Hearing your own supportive words can be enough to disrupt an old mindset.

You'll know your scripts are working when they appear automatically in moments of anxiety or self-doubt. Like a muscle, the habit strengthens with use. Eventually, you might react to a challenging situation by asking, "How can I try?" instead of shutting down. That's genuine progress—a rewiring that replaces doubt with possibility.

Give yourself space to play with language. Adjust scripts so they feel authentic. Plant them where you'll see them—mirrors, notebooks, or digital reminders. The more frequently you reach for these thought tools, the more instinctive they become. Soon, you'll notice your inner voice is less critical and more encouraging, and you'll find yourself more willing to act even when things get tough.

"FAIL FORWARD" RITUALS—TRANSFORMING SETBACKS INTO STEPPINGSTONES

Failure—the word alone can make your stomach clench, and your palms sweat. Whether it's a fizzled project, a bad grade, or an awkward conversation, we've all wanted to hide from our own mistake reel. But here's what resilient leaders and gritty teens learn: failure isn't the end. It's a rough draft on the road to growth. Adopting a "fail forward" mindset means treating setbacks as starting points, not stop signs. Instead of letting mistakes define you, you use them as personal tutors.

To "fail forward" is to see every misstep bringing you closer to a stronger, wiser self—one who can adapt, persist, and even find humor in the mess. With this approach, a failed side hustle or bad exam isn't doom; it's tuition in the school of progress. I once watched a friend spend months in a t-shirt business. When it flopped, she held a "failure party" to honor the lessons, realized her true passion was graphic design, and now freelances with dream clients.

The key is not letting setbacks linger and sour. Instead, create a simple ritual for handling failures—think emotional recycling. First, acknowledge what happened honestly and without drama. Maybe you missed a deadline or gave a flop presentation. Just say it: "That didn't go as planned." Next, reflect: What surprised you? What went wrong? How did you react? This isn't about blame—it's about observation.

Then, extract the lesson. Turn embarrassment into wisdom by asking, "What did I learn to help me next time?" Prepping your gym clothes the night before helps you stick to morning workouts, and last-minute studying is just gambling with grades. Once you spot any insight, plan your next action, even if it's small—set an earlier alarm, draft an outline, and get feedback before sharing.

Making It Practical: The Failure Reflection Journal

A simple way to make this stick is with a "failure reflection" journal. Use any notebook or scrap of paper. After a setback, write: What happened? How did it make me feel? What did I learn? What will I change next time? For example: "Missed two workouts. Felt frustrated but realized I needed phone reminders. Next week: set calendar alerts." When disappointment repeats, looking back on these entries can remind you that every flop carries a seed of progress.

Real Stories in Action

Consider Jamal, an aspiring entrepreneur whose first online gadget store launch bombed: almost no sales and awkward silence from friends. Instead of giving up, Jamal examined what went wrong (no marketing), studied digital advertising, and relaunched with better ads and messaging. The second attempt wasn't flawless, but his early setbacks became creative solutions.

Or Priya, a college student who failed her first chemistry midterm. Instead of quitting, she saw her professor, joined a study group, and realized she'd been memorizing, not practicing problems. She changed her study style. By finals, Priya was passing and tutoring classmates who once outperformed her.

Every comeback story starts with someone refusing to let failure be the last word. The magic lies in treating setbacks as materials for your next improvement. You become resilient by handling disappointment honestly and curiously rather than with shame.

Here's your prompt: After your next flop—big or small—grab a notebook or notes app and ask, "What did I learn here that I can use next time?" Write it down, even if it seems minor. You can celebrate the lesson: share it with a friend, reward yourself, or check it off as progress in your growth story.

BUILDING YOUR RESILIENCE PLAYBOOK—TOOLS FOR BOUNCING BACK

Do you know those days when you felt like a cell phone stuck at 2% battery? Or when your to-do list looks like a prank, and motivation is MIA? That's when you need more than wishful thinking—a resilience playbook. Think of it as your personal emergency kit for the emotional potholes and motivational flat tires that come with chasing big goals. Instead of scrambling for solutions in the heat of the moment, you'll have a stash of strategies ready to go. You're not just hoping for the best; you're setting yourself up to bounce back—ideally with less drama each time.

Start by building a few sections into your playbook. The first is self-care routines. These are not spa-day fantasies (unless you're into that, of course) but quick, realistic actions that restore your energy when you feel depleted. It could be stepping outside for fresh air, taking three slow breaths, or doing a 5-minute movement break. Science says that even brief physical activity—think walking around the block or some goofy dance moves—can reboot your mood and focus by increasing oxygen and happy brain chemicals. If moving feels impossible, try the "three good things" gratitude exercise: each night, write down three things that went right, no matter how small. It could be, "I didn't spill coffee on myself," "I replied to that scary email," or "My cat didn't knock over the plant today." Regularly focusing on positives rewires your brain's spotlight from stress to progress, which keeps burnout at bay.

The following section covers support contacts. Write down the names of two or three people who help you feel seen, encouraged, or less weird on tough days. Maybe it's a friend who texts memes when you mess up or a colleague who listens without fixing everything. List their phone numbers or usernames where you can see them. Sometimes, all it takes is reaching out with a quick "Motivation tank is empty—send help!" message. If you don't have people in your immediate circle, consider joining an accountability group or online community built around shared goals. Humans are social creatures; just knowing someone else cares can make setbacks sting a lot less.

Motivational reminders are your third playbook staple. These can be sticky notes with phrases that fire you up ("You survived worse Mondays!"), screenshots of encouraging DMs, or even short audio clips you record for yourself on good days. Don't underestimate the power of your voice cheering you on—the future you will thank the past you for the pep talk! Pin these reminders near your workspace or set them as phone alerts for when you usually get sidetracked.

Now, let's get tactical about burnout and discouragement because of those sneaky feelings like showing up uninvited. Take a few minutes and identify your top three warning signs that you're heading for trouble. Maybe you start doomscrolling, procrastinating on tasks, or snapping at innocent bystanders (sorry, barista). For each sign, pre-plan a counter-strategy—small actions that "interrupt" your downward spiral before it becomes a full-on slide. For instance, If I procrastinate, I'll text my accountability partner and confess what I'm avoiding. If I notice I haven't laughed all day, I'll watch a quick stand-up comedy clip. If my brain feels foggy after hours staring at screens,

I'll step outside or do ten jumping jacks (bonus points if you look ridiculous laughter is good medicine).

Your resilience playbook isn't just an idea to stash in your mental attic; it needs to live where you'll use it. Please print it out and tape it above your desk, keep it as a digital note pinned to your phone's home screen, or write it in the front of your planner. The easier it is to grab in a slump, the more likely you'll use it instead of spiraling into old habits. And don't treat this playbook as set in stone—update it as you discover what works (and what doesn't) for you. Maybe gratitude journaling felt cheesy at first but grew on you. Or perhaps calling someone right away isn't your style, but blasting energetic music is.

Remember, resilience isn't about never falling—it's about getting back up before inertia glues you to the floor. You're building muscle memory for bouncing back faster each time adversity takes a swing at you. Every tweak and update to your playbook personalizes it until it feels like a secret weapon no one else has. Keep this toolkit handy and let it evolve with you. The next time you hit a wall, reach for your playbook instead of allowing frustration to take the wheel. You'll be surprised how much easier it gets to regain momentum—and maybe even laugh at setbacks.

THE GROWTH MINDSET TRACKER—MEASURING CHANGE OVER TIME

Noticing changes in your thoughts is far more complicated than spotting a new haircut. That's why a growth mindset tracker is valuable—it's like a "progress mirror" for your brain. Instead of measuring only external successes, you use it to note the subtle but essential ways you respond to challenges and setbacks. Tracking these shifts proves that your thinking isn't fixed, helping you spot and reinforce positive changes before self-doubt sneaks back in.

Setting up a tracker is simple. Use a notebook, a notes app, or even a whiteboard—whatever fits your style. Make three columns: "Challenges Faced This Week," "My Mindset Response," and "New Belief

Formed." Each week, jot down challenging moments—maybe difficult feedback at work, learning something new, or facing a deadline. For each, record your immediate mental reaction. Did you freeze, or did you talk yourself through with patience? Lastly, note any new empowering belief you spotted, such as thinking, "I can do this if I break it down" instead of "I'm hopeless."

The magic comes when you make tracking a routine. Pick a regular time—Sunday night, Friday afternoon, or whenever you can quietly reflect. Review your week for moments that once stopped you but now seem less intimidating. For example, perhaps you avoided public-facing roles last month, but you volunteered to lead a meeting this week. Write that as a clear sign of shift. These small wins may not earn applause, but they matter as much as significant milestones.

Reflection goes beyond idle pondering—it's about recognizing your invisible wins and making them real. Use prompts like, "When did I surprise myself by reacting positively to a challenge?" or "What fear did I brush aside this week?" Perhaps you asked for help without anxiety or shrugged off criticism that once ruined your day. These are signs of real progress and deserve recognition. As weeks pass, your tracker will reveal patterns—maybe your self-talk grows gentler, or you take more risks without obsessing over the results.

Tracking your mindset also nudges you to experiment. Reviewing your week naturally leads you to look for ways to test new beliefs. This playful curiosity is one of the best ways to build resilience and self-trust, allowing you to see yourself as a scientist and subject in your development.

Don't keep these wins to yourself. Share them with someone supportive—an accountability partner, a mastermind group, or an online growth community. Post your top mindset win of the week, encourage others to share, or read what others are discovering. There's power in saying, "I handled that better than expected," or "I saw myself as a resilient learner today." Positive peer pressure can encourage even more growth.

If you struggle to be consistent—common when life gets busy—set reminders on your phone or calendar. Choose playful labels like "Mindset Check-in: Time to Brag!" or "Celebrate Your Brain Gains!" The goal is consistency, not perfection. If you skip a week, start again. Every entry builds your sense of improvement.

What's most rewarding is witnessing your identity shift—from someone who reacts to someone who intentionally shapes your mindset. You'll gather proof that old stories like "I always freeze under pressure" aren't as accurate anymore. You'll find it easier to take risks, and negative self-talk will diminish.

In sum, your mindset is flexible and evolving. Tracking growth makes progress visible, even when it feels slow. You're forming the mental habits and self-image of someone who perseveres, adapts, and learns through every experience. With greater self-awareness, you're ready to put your growing mindset into focused action on the road from vision to victory.

The difference between successful people and very successful people is that very successful people say 'no' to almost everything.

— WARREN BUFFETT

4

THE ART OF FOCUS— PRIORITIZING WHAT TRULY MOVES THE NEEDLE

THE "ONE THING" FILTER—CHOOSING THE GOAL THAT MATTERS MOST RIGHT NOW

Let's play a quick game of "Guess What's Actually Moving the Needle." Picture your to-do list as a buffet. Everything looks tempting—career leaps, marathon medals, new hobbies, maybe even learning French so you can finally order more than a baguette in Paris. You load up your plate but soon realize you're too full, and nothing tastes great. This happens when you try to chase too many goals at once. Do you feel busy but real progress? Not so much. That's where the "One Thing" Filter comes in—a decision-making lens for finding the single pursuit that creates the juiciest results with the least regret.

Here's the core question: "What's the one thing I can do that makes everything else easier or unnecessary?" This isn't just a clever slogan—it's a filter that forces you to confront which ambition will spark a domino effect in your life. Instead of spreading yourself thin, you pour your energy into the choice that creates positive ripples. Focusing on a single, high-impact goal multiplies your results because it avoids the trap of shallow multitasking and scattered effort. When your attention is diffused across five projects, everything crawls. But momentum builds when you go all-in on one thing, and outcomes accelerate.

Let's get practical. Suppose you're starting down three goals: switching careers, running a marathon, and learning French. All are worthy, but you can't give them equal weight without losing steam. It's time to evaluate them with a simple worksheet. List each goal, then score them on three scales: impact (how much it transforms your life), urgency (how soon it needs attention), and alignment (how closely it fits your values or long-term vision). Use a 1–5 scale for each category.

For example, let's fill out a sample worksheet:

Goal Impact (1-5) | **Urgency** (1-5) | **Alignment** (1-5) = **Total Score**
Career change 5,4,5= 14
Marathon training 3,2,4= 9
Learning French 2,1,3= 6

With this ranking, the career change wins by a landslide. It scores highest for impact and alignment—it will transform daily life and match core values. The marathon and French lessons might still be important, but they don't offer as much leverage. This doesn't mean you're giving up on them forever; it just means you're sequencing them for later, so you don't get overwhelmed and under-satisfied.

Now, let's talk about why narrowing down feels so slippery for most people: the dreaded FOMO—fear of missing out. You worry that if you pick one goal, you're automatically failing at everything else. That's a sneaky lie your brain tells you. The truth? Sequencing is your friend. You can do everything—but not all at once. If you commit deeply to one project for a season, you'll get more done over time than if you try to juggle everything simultaneously and drop the ball on all fronts.

People often stumble here by thinking they must choose their "forever goal" and give up their future flexibility. That's not how this works. Permit yourself to focus on one thing for a set window—a 90-day commitment challenge. Pour your best effort into your top-ranked goal for the next three months. If life changes or something else becomes urgent, revisit your priorities at the end of that period and adjust as needed.

Interactive Exercise: The "One Thing" Commitment Challenge

Grab a piece of paper or open your favorite notes app. List three goals fighting for your attention right now. For each, score impact (1–5), urgency (1–5), and alignment (1–5). Total the scores. Circle the highest one—this is your "One Thing" for the next 90 days. Write down one action you'll take this week to move it forward and one reward you'll give yourself if you stick with it until the end of your commitment window.

If you start to feel that old itch of wanting to do everything at once, remind yourself that real Focus is an act of confidence, not limitation. The more intentional you become about sequencing your ambitions, the more satisfying each victory feels—and the more likely you are to enjoy that croissant in Paris someday, French accent optional.

THE EISENHOWER MATRIX HACK—SEPARATING URGENT FROM IMPORTANT

Let's be honest—your to-do list often seems to multiply independently. One minute, you feel on top of things; the next, you're swamped by "urgent" emails, overdue forms, a needy dog, and reminders to call Aunt Martha. Feeling overwhelmed is common, but the Eisenhower Matrix offers a practical solution. Developed by President Dwight D. Eisenhower, this tool helps you organize tasks into four categories: (1) urgent and essential, (2) important but not urgent, (3) urgent but not necessary, and (4) neither urgent nor essential. Picture a simple 2×2 grid: "urgent" vs. "not urgent" on one axis; "important" vs. "not important" on the other. Everything you do fits somewhere in that grid—even "watch cat videos until noon."

The key here is realizing that urgency isn't the same as importance. Most people spend their days reacting to urgent tasks—deadlines, crises, drama—while neglecting what's important, like building skills, planning your career, or meaningful projects. If you treat everything urgent as necessary, you'll always be reactive, never focusing on actions that lead to real progress or big wins.

Try it yourself: draw four quadrants on paper or a device. Jot down your tasks, big and small: reply to emails, update your resume, work on your website portfolio, schedule a checkup, pay phone bills, renew your license, bake cookies, and binge-watch a show. Now, sort them. "Urgent and important" might be renewing your license before it expires. "Important but not urgent" covers work like portfolio-building or learning a new skill—things that matter long-term but aren't crises. "Urgent but not important" are distractions that demand quick responses but bring little value, like the relentless wave of emails or last-minute, low-stakes requests. "Not urgent and not important" are your time drains, like endless social scrolling or re-organizing your sock drawer.

The real benefit comes from handling each category with intention. Quadrant 1—urgent and important—are the true emergencies.

Handle these first but aim to spend less time here to avoid burnout. Quadrant 2—important but not urgent—is where proactive growth happens. Regularly schedule time for these crucial but quiet tasks: deep learning, future planning, and prepping presentations early. This is how you move forward instead of scrambling from crisis to crisis.

Quadrants 3 and 4 are where time disappears. "Urgent but not important" tasks masquerade as priorities but rarely help you progress— delegate, minimize, or set strict time limits for them. Use quick replies, auto-responders, or templates to handle these efficiently. As for "not urgent and not important," be ruthless: unsubscribe from emails you never read, batch chores, and automate bill payments to reduce their impact.

Visual Guide: Eisenhower Matrix Sample

Urgent & Important (renew license)	Important/Not Urgent (build portfolio)
Urgent/Not Important (reply to random emails)	Not Urgent/Not Important (cat video marathon)

You'll notice a sense of control as you consistently use this matrix. You'll quickly recognize which fires are legitimate and which are just smoke. The guilt over ignoring distractions fades as you understand where your attention belongs. With time, sorting tasks into these quadrants becomes second nature, and you'll navigate choices with more confidence and less stress.

A final tip: fiercely protect your Quadrant 2 time. Block off at least an hour each week for important but not urgent priorities, treating it as non-negotiable as brushing your teeth. Even during busy weeks, maintaining this habit keeps you focused on actual progress instead of being consumed by other people's urgent demands.

The Eisenhower Matrix isn't just for executives or productivity buffs —students, new managers, or anyone feeling scattered will benefit from it. Don't let urgency dictate every action. Use this system to identify what matters and move stalled priorities off the back burner for good.

BRAIN DUMP TO ACTION PLAN—CLEARING MENTAL CLUTTER FAST

Ever feel like your brain is a whiteboard at the end of a wild brain-storming meeting—random doodles, half-formed ideas, and a grocery list hiding in the corner? Welcome to the club. Focus disappears when your mind buzzes with a thousand reminders, worries, and to-dos. That's precisely why I'm a fan of the brain dump. This simple exercise is my go-to for cleaning the house upstairs. All you need is a timer, somewhere to write (paper or your favorite notes app), and a willingness to let it all spill out—no filter, no shame. Set your timer for ten minutes. Challenge yourself to jot down everything on your mind, whether trivial or bizarre. Work deadlines, dentist appointments, "remember to buy socks," "call Grandma," "start that podcast," "worry about climate change," "figure out what's for dinner"—dump it all out. The goal isn't organization yet; it's evacuation. Treat this like mental spring cleaning: everything must go, at least for now.

Staring at this mountain of scribbles after your timer dings can initially feel overwhelming but trust me—chaos on paper beats chaos in your head every time. Now comes the satisfying part: sorting through the mess and giving each thought a new home. I use three categories: actionable (something you must do), delegable or automatable (something someone else or a digital tool could handle), and discardable (stuff you don't need to worry about). Here's what that might look like in action:

Action Now, Delegate/Automate, Let Go

Finish project report	Action Now
Grocery delivery app	Delegate/Automate
Worrying about Pluto	Let Go
Email boss	Delegate/Automate
Schedule car service	Action Now
Remembering 8th-grade PE	Delegate/Automate
Pay phone bill	Delegate/Automate
That thing from 2013	Let Go

You'll be amazed at how much lighter your brain feels just seeing things in these buckets. For anything in the "Action Now" pile, break it down into bite-sized steps and build a simple action plan. I keep it easy: write down the task, assign a date (or at least a general time-frame), and jot down the following action required. Take "Finish project report." The next step could be "Outline main points" scheduled for Thursday, then "Draft intro" on Friday. If "Email boss" is hanging over you, set a calendar reminder for tomorrow at 9:00 a.m., type a draft now, or at least write the first sentence so there's zero friction when you open your inbox.

Here's an action plan template I love using:

Task	Date	Time	Next Step	Follow up
Proposal	Monday	10am	Draft	Reply email
Schedule checkup	Tuesday	11am	Call doctor office	
Pay phone bill	Friday	3pm	Log in provider app	

Keep it visible—on your fridge, in your planner, or as a widget on your phone's home screen. The trick is to make the next steps so obvious that procrastination doesn't stand a chance. For anything in the "Delegate/Automate" category, ask yourself: Can I text someone right now to take this off my plate? Would a calendar alert or automation tool save me time? For example, setting up auto-pay for bills or using a meal delivery app for groceries can free up precious mental energy for more meaningful work.

Now, let's be real—some items belong in the "Let Go" pile for good reason. Not everything deserves space in your head. If you agonize over an old embarrassment or worry about things you can't control (like Pluto's planetary status), cross it off with gusto. You're not being irresponsible; you're protecting your Focus.

I recommend making brain dumps a weekly ritual. Sunday night works for me—it feels like taking out the trash before starting fresh on Monday. Set a calendar reminder and treat it like non-negotiable self-care. Ten minutes once a week can save you hours of spinning your wheels later.

If you want to take it up a notch, add some flair: colored pens for categories, stickers for completed actions, or voice notes if you think faster than you type. If you're into tech, apps like Notion or Google Keep let you tag and search entries later. For those who crave accountability, pair up with a friend and exchange "top three actions" post-brain-dump each week.

The beauty of this practice isn't just feeling less scattered—it's about creating clarity so you can spot what truly deserves attention. Your brain stops buzzing with background noise, and suddenly, those big goals start looking more approachable. A regular brain dump turns mental chaos into clear steps and—best of all—gives you permission to stop carrying every little thing around all day long.

OVERCOMING COMPARISON TRAPS—STAYING IN YOUR OWN LANE

Ever scroll through your feed and feel like everyone else is thriving while you're just trying to keep your plants alive? Welcome to the comparison trap. Social media has turned comparison into a nonstop game, giving us curated highlight reels full of vacations, achievements, and filtered snapshots. Instead of feeling inspired, you might feel stuck, behind, or invisible. It's wild how a few moments spent scrolling can make you question your progress—or wonder if you're moving. This isn't just an occasional annoyance. Constant comparison eats away at self-confidence and Focus, leaving you with the sense of falling behind. Your accomplishments shrink next to the curated lives of others, and the gap between your reality and their "feed-worthy" moments grows.

The first step to breaking free is figuring out your triggers. Everyone has something or someone that sets off those "not enough" feelings, whether it's a coworker who gets every promotion, a friend's 6 a.m. workout selfies, or endless success stories on LinkedIn. Maybe you feel it after seeing certain Instagram accounts, an old rival's updates, or even a family member's "helpful" feedback that stings more than support. Reflect honestly: What—or who—consistently leaves you feeling "less than"? Write it out, no sugarcoating. Knowing your comparison triggers isn't about blame—it's about clarity. Once you understand where envy sneaks in, you can redirect your energy.

Now, shift your Focus: Instead of pouring energy into comparison, channel it toward your growth. Start a "progress journal" just for yourself. Write down every win, no matter how small: sending a tough email, finishing a project, making time for a workout, or avoiding an online argument. This isn't bragging—it's proof you're moving forward in ways meaningful to you. The more visibly you track your own growth, the less validating strangers' highlight reels will appear. Turn off push notifications during focus times—remind yourself you're not missing out by tuning into your own frequency.

Comparison thrives where showmanship is prioritized over substance, so curating your environment is essential. Online, unfollow or mute any account that triggers insecurity or distraction. Replace them with voices that inspire genuine growth, not competition. Make a "role model" list—people who motivate you by sharing lessons, effort, and resilience, not just glossy successes. Offline, surround yourself with friends and mentors who cheer you on without keeping score. If someone's achievements consistently make you feel worse, consider taking a break from that connection or setting more precise boundaries.

A digital detox is sometimes the best solution—log off for a weekend. The internet will continue without you, and so will you. Use this time to reconnect with what brings you joy—reading, hiking, trying new recipes, or just catching up on sleep. When you return online, notice how much less urgent other people's updates seem.

Comparison won't disappear; it's part of being human. But you can always choose where to focus your energy. Every time you feel yourself slipping into envy or self-doubt, shift your perspective: What can you do today to build your highlight reel? Celebrate your wins, even quietly or with a friend who understands. With practice, you'll spend less time watching others' races and more time running your own—at your pace and in your way.

Reflection Prompt

Write down three accounts or situations that regularly trigger comparison for you. Next to each, list one step you'll take this week to minimize its impact—maybe it's muting an account, skipping a weekly scroll, or countering negative self-talk with a reminder of your recent achievement. End by noting one thing you genuinely appreciate about your current path—no matter how simple.

SETTING BOUNDARIES FOR DEEP WORK—PROTECTING FOCUS IN A DISTRACTED WORLD

Imagine your brain as a computer overloaded with open tabs: some play music, others bombard you with pop-ups, and a few are stuck on distracting videos. Now try coding or writing a research paper amid that chaos—progress slows to a crawl. This is why "deep work" is so valuable. Deep work is time set aside for entirely focused, meaningful effort, free from distractions. Cal Newport made this concept popular, explaining that our best ideas and work happen when we avoid interruptions for at least an hour or two at a time. By contrast, "shallow work" (responding to emails, mindlessly scrolling, constant notifications) may keep us busy but rarely produces enduring results (Sinek, 2017).

Most environments aren't naturally built for deep work. Distractions are everywhere—be it a buzzing phone, a knock on the door, or even your mind drifting off to mundane reminders. One helpful method to become aware of these distractions is keeping a "distraction log." For a set work session, jot down every interruption, whether an external ping or an internal urge. Review your notes afterward, and you'll see patterns: maybe it's constant email pop-ups or noise leaking in from another room.

Once you know where your Focus breaks down, it's time to shore up the weak spots. One major obstacle can be others not respecting your quiet time, especially in shared spaces or at home. The solution is simple, direct communication and minor environmental adjustments. Don't assume people will notice your needs—tell them: "I'll be working from 9 to 11; can we talk after?" It may feel awkward initially, but most are receptive if you're clear. A "Do Not Disturb" sign or a closed door works wonders for roommates or family. In open offices or noisy places, noise-canceling headphones can help—even if you're playing white noise.

Digital distractions are a major culprit for most people. Out of sight, out of mind: put your phone away or flip it face down. Tools like Freedom or Cold Turkey block time-wasting websites so you can focus guilt-free. Turn off notifications completely or use your device's "focus mode"—the change in your attention, even for ten minutes, is noticeable. Try creating a "focus zone" by keeping only necessary items in view and clearing clutter or unrelated tasks from your workspace.

You must experiment to find your ideal routine. Some people thrive with big morning focus blocks; others do better with short sprints (25 minutes on, five minutes off). Block deep work sessions on your calendar and treat them like essential appointments. If you're worried about others misinterpreting your silence, explain your schedule to colleagues or friends so they know you're being intentional—not rude.

Minor environmental tweaks help, too. If noise is distracting, try background music, ambient, or white noise. Rearranging your space to face away from foot traffic can minimize visual distractions. Tell a friend when you start a deep work block for accountability and ask them to check your progress.

Protecting your Focus isn't just about efficiency—it's about forming a habit of honoring your commitments to yourself. A few successful deep work sessions remind you how rewarding proper Focus feels. It's like clearing static to hear a favorite song finally.

To summarize, Focus isn't about extreme discipline but protecting your attention through smart boundaries and simple routines. Once you normalize defending focus time and communicating your needs, you'll find it easier to progress on projects that matter. Deep work isn't just another productivity trend; it's a crucial tool for turning big ideas into real-world wins.

Next, we'll examine how habits and motivation keep this focused effort alive for the long run.

MAKE A DIFFERENCE
WITH YOUR REVIEW

UNLOCK THE POWER OF GENEROSITY

"The best way to find yourself is to lose yourself in the service of others."

— MAHATMA GANDHI

Ever feel like your brain has 47 tabs open, four frozen, and music playing from somewhere? You're not alone. Most people are overwhelmed before they even start. That's exactly why I wrote *UNSTUCK*—to help folks like us find clarity, set real goals, and actually finish what matters.

Now I need your help.

Would you take one minute to leave a review? It's totally free, takes less than a minute, and can help someone else get *unstuck* too.

Most people pick books based on what others say. Your review could help someone just like you—busy, overloaded, and looking for a place to start.

Your kind words could help…

- one more dreamer pick their first goal
- one more parent carve out time for themselves
- one more burned-out adult find hope
- one more person learn to *say no* to the noise
- one more life change, just by starting with one step

▤ Just scan this QR code and leave your review:

Or visit: https://www.amazon.com/review/review-your-purchases?asin=B0FJFJM6SP

If you're someone who likes to lift others up—you're my kind of person.

Thanks for helping make someone else's fresh start possible.

– Valarie V. Henry

Author of *UNSTUCK*

Start where you are. Use what you have. Do what you can.

— ARTHUR ASHE

5

GOAL DESIGN—BREAKING AMBITIONS INTO ACTIONABLE PIECES

FROM DREAM TO DEADLINE—REVERSE ENGINEERING YOUR GOAL

I magine facing a vast, chaotic Lego set: the finished castle looks great on the box, but the messy pile in front of you is overwhelming. That's how big goals often feel—impressive in theory but confusing. The twist? You don't have to build from the bottom up. The most effective approach is to start with the finished product in mind and then break it into manageable parts you can tackle. This is the essence of reverse engineering your goal—thinking like an architect who sketches the blueprint before picking up a hammer.

Reverse engineering means starting with your ideal result and mapping your way backward to where you stand now. Suppose your goal is to publish a book. Don't simply declare, "I'll write a book this year," and wait for inspiration (speaking from experience: December comes quickly, and all you have are ideas and snacks). Instead, draw a timeline. On the far right, write "Book Launch Day." Work in reverse: just before the launch is "final edits done," before that "beta readers review," then "first draft finished," and so on back to "decided to write a book." You've just created a flowchart that turns goal confusion into Clarity.

Let's break this into stages. Nearly all big goals have natural phases—a sequence guiding you from unsure to accomplished. To launch a side business, write your finish line: "Business opens." Then backtrack: "Website live," "filed legal paperwork," "branding set," "product developed," "market research done," back to "idea sketched." Each phase should feel distinct and manageable—don't overwhelm yourself by lumping too much into one step.

Next, define milestones for each phase. Think of milestones as checkpoints in a video game—they confirm your progress and provide motivation. For writing a book, milestones could be: "completed research," "wrote chapter one," "hit 20,000 words," and "sent the manuscript to an editor." For a business: "surveyed 50 potential customers," "secured business name," "first sale made." These aren't arbitrary; they're objective progress markers.

Deadlines make your plan concrete. Don't just guess—"I'll finish this in two weeks!"—as random deadlines often lead to frustration. Instead, research how long each phase takes or ask experienced people. If you're training for a half-marathon, see if most plans require 12 weeks. Building a website? Check with someone who's done it or look up average timeframes. Review your schedule honestly: do you have two hours a week or ten? Adjust the plan for your real-life commitments—work, school, or Netflix binges.

Now, create your goal roadmap. This simple, visual plan shows each step on your journey—not just the destination. For example:

Goal Roadmap

Phase/Stage	Start Date	End Date	Milestone/Deliverable
Research	Apr 1	Apr 7	Competitor analysis completed
Branding	Apr 8	Apr 15	Logo and colors finalized
Website Development	Apr 16	Apr 30	Website live
Product Prep	May 1	May 14	First batch ready
Launch Prep	May 15	May 28	Social media scheduled
Launch	May 29	May 29	First customer call scheduled

Each phase has precise dates and a specific deliverable—no gray areas, just actionable steps you can check off. You don't need perfection here; the goal is Clarity. Post this roadmap above your desk or keep it on your phone as a daily reminder that steady progress is possible.

Interactive Exercise: Build Your Reverse-Engineered Roadmap

Take some sticky notes or open a notes app. Write your end goal on one note at the far right. On others, list each key phase needed to reach it, working backward to today. Under each phase, jot down one milestone and a realistic deadline. Arrange the notes in order—now you have a clear step-by-step plan tailored to your life.

Reverse engineering isn't flashy—it's innovative and practical. The process becomes far less intimidating by breaking down your goal into logical phases with real deadlines supported by research. Now, with a clear path ahead, each step feels manageable—no longer like staring at an endless pile of Legos.

THE MICRO-MILESTONE METHOD—CELEBRATING WINS ALONG THE WAY

Let's be honest: huge goals have a sneaky way of morphing from exciting to intimidating the moment you try to start. Staring at a giant ambition—finishing a degree, running a half-marathon, launching a podcast—can make even the most motivated person want to crawl under a blanket and binge snacks instead. That's why micro-milestones exist. Imagine your big goal is a mountain. Micro-milestones are the colorful flags you plant along the way, each one a mini celebration that says, "Hey, I'm still moving!" Instead of waiting months (or years) for a central finish line, you build motivation by racking up small, frequent wins. These mini checkpoints aren't just for fun—psychologists have shown that celebrating progress boosts dopamine and keeps you returning for more. When your brain gets that little hit of "I did it!" you stay engaged instead of burning out halfway up the mountain.

Micro-milestones are the "bite-sized" goals nestled inside each bigger phase. Picture you're tackling a fitness goal. Instead of measuring success only by "run a 10K," you mark every step: "ran 5 minutes without stopping," "completed workout number one," "stretched three days in a row." Each one is a legitimate victory, not just filler. For creative projects, break things down similarly: "outlined chapter one," "wrote 500 words for five days straight," and "shared first draft with a friend." The trick is to make each micro-milestone clear and achievable in a short time frame. You want them so doable that you can't help but rack up momentum—even when energy is low, or the couch looks extra inviting.

Documenting your progress isn't just for type-A planners or people with fancy notebooks. It's for anyone who wants to see their momentum, not just hope it's happening. Progress bars, checklists, and trackers are your new best friends. You could grab some sticky notes and slap them on your wall—one for every micro-milestone. Or print out a tracker with boxes to color in after every win (bonus: coloring is oddly satisfying). If digital is your jam, use an app with celebratory confetti animations or a simple spreadsheet with columns for each milestone. Some people take progress selfies at each checkpoint, while others use habit tracker apps that reward streaks. There's no single right way—find a system that feels playful or motivating, so it gets used.

Rewards matter more than you think—and no, they don't have to break the bank or wreck your schedule. Set up tiny treats for every micro-milestone hit. Run five minutes without stopping? Queue up your favorite playlist for tomorrow's workout. Finish a whole week of study sessions? Grab coffee with a friend or indulge in that guilty-pleasure show guilt-free. Some folks build a "Wins Wall"—a real or virtual gallery of proof that they are progressing. Each time you reach a checkpoint, snap a quick photo or leave yourself a funny sticky note about how awesome you are. These little rewards might seem silly, but they train your brain to connect effort with positive feelings, making it much easier to stick with your plan when life gets chaotic.

The psychological magic here is rooted in reinforcement learning—a fancy term for "do a good thing, get a good feeling, want to do more good things." When you tie visible progress and small rewards to each step, your brain craves the successive win instead of dreading the next hurdle. This method works for every kind of goal: learning guitar gets easier when you celebrate playing two songs without mistakes; saving money feels less like deprivation when you pat yourself on the back after hitting each $100 milestone. Even tackling scary tasks like giving presentations becomes less terrifying when you acknowledge every mini accomplishment along the way.

Don't overlook the social side of celebrating micro-milestones, either. Sharing your mini wins with friends or accountability partners boosts motivation even more. Text someone your progress, post in an online group, or brag to your pet (they're great listeners). Positive feedback amplifies your achievements, making the process enjoyable and less lonely. If you're feeling creative, invent fun rituals for each checkpoint —maybe a victory dance in your kitchen or a dramatic reading of your progress from the bathroom mirror.

The real secret of the micro-milestone method is that it makes every day feel like progress day—not just those rare moments when everything lines up perfectly. It turns big, intimidating goals into a series of tiny victories so achievable that you start to believe finishing is not just possible but inevitable. And the best part? You'll have way more reasons to celebrate along the way—not just at the end when everyone else finally notices what you've accomplished.

ACTION STEP MAPPING—TRANSLATING AMBITION INTO WEEKLY TO-DOS

You've got your goal mapped out, your micro-milestones are ready to roll, and you feel like a human-made motivational poster. But here's where reality steps in—unless you break those milestones into actual, tiny actions for this week (not "someday" or "soon"), your plan is just a well-dressed wish. The magic happens when you move ambitions out of your head and onto your calendar. This is where action step mapping saves the day. Think of it like translating a foreign language: you're taking "big dream speak" and converting it into "what can I actually do between Wednesday's lunch meeting and Thursday's Netflix marathon?" That means every micro-milestone needs to be broken down into clear, specific tasks you can check off before the weekend hits.

The trick is to get uncomfortably specific—vague intentions are sneaky goal-killers. Instead of writing "network more," try "Research three local networking events by Friday." Planning to write a novel? "Write 300 words daily, five days this week" is your bread and butter. If you want to update your resume, don't just stick "update resume" on a sticky note and hope for the best. Try "brainstorm three new bullet points for work experience on Monday." You're not just making lists—creating a playbook for your week, that leaves zero room for confusion. Clarity beats willpower every time.

To keep the wheels turning, use a weekly action planner. This doesn't need to be fancy. A simple grid does the trick, with columns for the date, your action step, its priority (high, medium, low), and whether you finished it or want to roll it over.

Here's how it might look:

Date	Task	Priority	Outcome
7/1	Brainstorm 3 resume bullet points	high	
7/2	Write 300 words for blog	medium	
7/3	Reach out to one potential mentor by noon	high	
7/4	Research two networking events	low	
7/5	Edit blog draft	medium	

You fill in those outcomes at the end of each day—check marks feel amazing, trust me. If a task lingers untouched, scoot it forward or shrink it until it's bite-sized enough that you'll do it even on your most distracted day. The secret sauce is "right-sizing." Life is busy. You need tasks so small they're almost impossible to put off. If "prepare presentation" feels like Everest, break it into "draft key talking points for five minutes on Wednesday morning." Have a big research paper? Schedule "find two relevant articles before dinner on Tuesday." You want actions that fit inside one sitting or less—think single-serving, not buffet.

The beauty of this approach is its flexibility. Not every week will be smooth. Some days explode with emergencies or unexpected dog hair emergencies (yes, those happen). If you try to power through giant tasks during chaos, you'll end up overwhelmed. Shrink the step and keep the momentum alive. This is productivity's best-kept secret: small progress almost always beats sporadic, heroic effort.

Now, don't just plow through without looking back. The end-of-week review is where the real growth sneaks in. Take ten minutes each Sunday night or Monday morning to reflect: What did I finish? What tripped me up? What can I tweak for next week? Ask yourself, "What was my biggest win?"—celebrate it, even if it was just sending one awkward email or resisting the siren call of social media for an hour. Then ask, "What needs to change?" Maybe you aimed too high or forgot to schedule downtime. Adjust your planner accordingly, guilt-free.

This ritual isn't about perfection; it's about building awareness and confidence in your process. If you notice some tasks keep rolling over week after week, that's a clue: either break them down further or question if they really matter right now. Weekly review isn't an interrogation—it's a friendly check-in with yourself. It turns planning into a living process that grows with you.

For those who love paper planners, block out your action steps in colored pens or stickers for added flair. Digital fans can set up recurring reminders in their favorite app—some even let you track streaks or add little fireworks when you check things off (every brain loves a tiny dopamine parade). The format doesn't matter as much as consistency: keep your plan visible and tweak as needed.

The final touch: keep action step mapping playful. If you miss a task, don't beat yourself up; resize it or swap it for something easier next time. This approach trains your brain to associate planning with progress—not punishment—and that's how real change sticks.

CREATING CONTINGENCY PLANS—ANTICIPATING AND NAVIGATING ROADBLOCKS

You know that feeling when you're riding a wave of motivation, only for life to throw a wrench in your plans—a flat tire, getting sick, or a surprise meeting? Most advice assumes things will go smoothly, but life is full of unexpected challenges. That's why contingency planning —the art of expecting the unexpected and prepping your responses— is key to finishing what you start. It's not just for the ultra-organized; it's a practical tool for anyone serious about their goals. With backup plans, you're ready to respond calmly when things go wrong instead of scrambling to get back on track.

Think of contingency planning as making your own detour signs. If you're training for a race and bad weather hits, you've prepped indoor workouts. If you're working on a creative project and get stuck, you have prompts or a playlist ready. The point isn't to obsess over every possible disaster but to identify the three obstacles most likely to block your progress and brainstorm at least two realistic, specific workarounds for each. Avoid vague solutions like "work harder"—list your steps. If a lack of time is the issue, your plans could be to "shorten my workout to 15 minutes" or "exercise before work instead of after." If motivation drops, maybe it's "text my accountability partner for support" or "read my Wins Wall for a quick boost." Make these responses so simple and accessible that you can use them even when running on empty.

A favorite tool for this is the "roadblock response card" system. Write each likely obstacle on an index card, sticky note, or phone note paired with your backup responses. Examples: "If I get sick, I'll switch to a gentle stretch and push my timeline back one week," or "If I hit a creative slump, I'll free-write for 15 minutes just to stay moving." Preparing for problems that haven't happened may feel awkward, but when things inevitably go sideways, you'll be glad to have solutions at your fingertips. Keep these visible—tape them inside your planner, by your workspace, or set reminders on your phone—so your Plan B is always handy.

To put this into practice, write your current goal in the center of a page. List three obstacles you've encountered before, or suspect could come up again. For each, brainstorm two realistic backup actions— not something superhuman, but things you'll do. For example, if you're prone to procrastination, your plans might be to "set a five-minute timer to just start" or "have someone check in on me at noon." For schedule derailments—like last-minute overtime or emergencies —your responses might be "move one task to the weekend" or "do a double session tomorrow." The more tailored these actions are to your lifestyle, the more likely they'll work when needed.

Remember, this isn't a set-it-and-forget-it process. Life changes, bringing new obstacles and challenges. That's why it's smart to revisit your contingency plans monthly. Set a recurring "Contingency Review" reminder to reflect on what's working, what isn't, and what needs to change. Your original workaround isn't practical, or you have new challenges like unexpected school projects or deadlines. Use this time to update your cards, add obstacles, and brainstorm new solutions. This isn't about predicting every problem but about building resilience and getting comfortable with the reality that setbacks don't equal failure—they mean it's time to adjust your approach.

Proactively planning for setbacks makes staying on track about luck and more about skill. The real benefit? When obstacles hit, you won't waste energy panicking or giving up—you'll know what to do next. Contingency planning is like giving future-you a head start, turning would-be dead ends into manageable speed bumps. You may never avoid every bump (unless you can control the weather), but having a solid Plan B—and C—means you'll always keep moving forward, even if you must take a slightly different route to get there.

THE "PIVOT PROTOCOL"—ADJUSTING GOALS WITHOUT LOSING MOMENTUM

Here's a secret: real-life progress rarely travels in a straight line. Sometimes, your big, shiny goal makes sense at first—then life throws a curveball, your motivation shifts, or your knees start negotiating new terms (thanks, marathon training). That's when the "Pivot Protocol" enters the chat. This isn't about quitting or failure. The Pivot Protocol is a structured approach for reevaluating and resetting goals with purpose, so you keep moving forward even when the original plan no longer fits. Think of it as your personal reset button that doesn't erase your progress or spirit but helps you course-correct with confidence.

Start with an honest check-in. Step one: ask yourself, "What's changed?" Maybe your work schedule exploded, your body sent new signals, or your interests evolved. This isn't about blaming yourself for losing steam; it's about recognizing that circumstances, health, and priorities are living, breathing things. Step two: pinpoint what's not working. Maybe you're forcing yourself into morning runs your dread, or your creative project has become a burden instead of a joy.

Name the friction without sugarcoating it. Step three: clarify what matters now. What feels meaningful? What fits your current bandwidth and brings excitement—or at least makes sense for this season? If your goal was to run a marathon, but your knees have started issuing threats, maybe daily walking or swimming emerges as a better fit. The pivot isn't giving up; it's updating your ambitions to match who you are today.

Now, guilt often creeps in here—especially if you've told people about your goal or have partners counting on you. That's normal, but you don't have to carry it alone. Communicating your pivot can feel awkward, but it doesn't have to be a dramatic confession. Try a script like, "After checking in with myself, I've realized my priorities and energy are shifting. I'm focusing on something that fits my current season better." If you're working with an accountability partner or a team, add, "Here's how I plan to keep growing: [insert new goal or focus]." This approach takes the pressure off perfection and puts the spotlight on growth and honesty.

Don't forget—adaptability is a form of strength, not weakness. Changing direction doesn't erase all the work you've put in; instead, it proves you're willing to listen to reality and act accordingly. Celebrate persistence in a new direction just as much as sticking to the original plan. Share your "pivot win" with your support crew or post about it in a community space dedicated to goal-getters. A "pivot win" could be anything from swapping out marathon training for daily walks and feeling more energized to shifting from creating YouTube videos (which made you want to throw your laptop out the window) to podcasting, which feels genuinely fun and sustainable.

Here's an exercise: Block out time this week for a "Pivot Protocol" review. Journal on these prompts—What has changed in my life or motivation recently? Which part of my goal feels off? What new version of this goal excites me or fits my needs better? Afterward, draft a short message for anyone needing an update on your new direction. Even if you never send it, writing helps release guilt and makes the new path feel official.

It's easy to see pivots as embarrassing detours, but they are signs of wisdom and grit. The Pivot Protocol helps you respond with intention when life doesn't go as planned. It's about ditching old blueprints that no longer fit and building something that works right now. Every time you pivot thoughtfully and share your process (even with yourself), you reinforce that progress isn't a straight shot but a winding path full of smart adjustments.

Wrapping up this chapter: Goal design isn't just about getting from Point A to Point B—it's about building a flexible roadmap for real life. Whether reverse engineering deadlines, celebrating micro-wins, mapping action steps, prepping for obstacles, or pivoting with pride, you're setting yourself up for sustainable success. Next, we'll explore what it takes to keep momentum strong over the long haul—because finishing well matters just as much as starting smart.

Success isn't always about greatness. It's about consistency. Consistent hard work gains success. Greatness will come.

— DWAYNE "THE ROCK" JOHNSON

6

MASTERING MOTIVATION —BUILDING HABITS AND ENERGY FOR THE LONG HAUL

THE MOTIVATION MONDAY RITUAL—KICKSTARTING EACH WEEK WITH INTENTION

Mondays are often seen as the villain of the week: "Ugh, it's Monday," people sigh, blaming it for every bad mood and mishap. But what if Mondays became your secret weapon for chasing your goals? Imagine making Monday a day to reboot your focus and motivation, like hitting "refresh" on your browser.

There's science behind this feeling. Psychologists call it the "Monday effect"—people feel more hopeful and committed to change at the start of a week. Mondays act as a natural reset, which is why gyms fill up and planners come out, and why so many of us promise, "I'll start next week." Even after a rough patch, Monday lets you reset and try again. That's a surprisingly valuable opportunity!

The trick is using this psychological window to fuel your progress. Enter the Motivation Monday Ritual. Think of this as a personal pep rally—no awkward chanting required. The goal: set an intention for the week, remind yourself what matters, and spark enough energy to carry you past midweek slumps. It's not about perfection or overloaded to-do lists, but about reconnecting with your priorities and giving yourself a solid launchpad.

Begin with a morning check-in. Grab your favorite drink, find a quiet spot (or the closest you can get), and take five minutes to journal. Ask: What do I want this week to feel like? What's one thing I'm excited to tackle? Jot down your top priority—just one. This could be "finish my project proposal," "run twice," or even "survive three Zoom meetings without turning into a meme." That's your anchor.

Then, update your Wins Wall or progress tracker. Log any wins—from sending that dreaded email to watering your plants. Celebrating even tiny victories trains your brain to crave progress. Keep these visible: sticky notes, a bulletin board, or a selfie to mark an accomplishment.

Boost your energy next. Play a song that helps you wake up, even if it's just chair-dancing with coffee. Watch an inspirational video or record a short voice memo for your future self: "You're awesome. You can totally handle that presentation." If you have an accountability buddy, swap short notes of encouragement to start the week together.

Personalization is key. Your Motivation Monday Ritual should feel rewarding, not like homework. If journaling isn't your thing, doodle your goals. If music doesn't help, read a quote or a poem. Some people light a candle or use aromatherapy; others take a quick walk outside.

Experiment until something genuinely fires you up. There's no wrong way—just find what works for you.

Motivation Monday Worksheet

Try this quick template—note it digitally:

Take a few quiet moments to ground yourself for the week ahead. Reflect, refocus, and reignite your drive.

• My top priority for this week:

_____

_____

_____

• One thing I'm genuinely excited for:

_____

_____

_____

• Last week's win I'm proud of:

_____

_____

_____

• My intention or theme for this week (one word):

_____

_____

_____

• What will make me smile today?

_____

_____

_____

Answer honestly. Keep it visible all week; snap a photo and use it as your phone wallpaper if you'd like.

No matter how busy life gets, returning to this ritual every Monday gives you a reliable reset—a psychological cue that says, "We're starting fresh!" Even in messy weeks, this can anchor you and rekindle your spark. Mix in new elements occasionally—a friend's pep talk, a meme, new music—to keep things fresh.

If Mondays don't fit your schedule (night shift or weekend work), pick another reliable reset day. The magic is in intentionally starting anew with purpose and positivity, not the day itself.

HABIT-BUILDING HACKS—FROM WILLPOWER TO AUTOMATIC ACTION

You know that feeling when you tell yourself, "I'll just use willpower," and then your brain laughs and hits snooze again? We all want to rely on sheer determination, but habits win the race. The good news: you don't need to be a superhero to make goal-getting automatic. It's about clever design, not brute force. One of my favorite tools is habit stacking. This trick is all about tacking a new habit onto an existing routine—no extra brainpower required. For example, if you already drink coffee each morning (and let's be honest, who doesn't?), you can pair that caffeine ritual with writing one sentence toward your novel or jotting down your daily goal. Maybe you brush your teeth at night; that's your cue to spend two minutes stretching or planning tomorrow's top task. The beauty is in the anchor—linking a new behavior to something you do without thinking.

Science backs this up. Habits form when you repeat the same behavior in response to a cue, then reward yourself—cue, routine, reward. That's the magic formula. The cue could be a visual trigger—a Post-it on your bathroom mirror yelling "Plank for 30 seconds!" The routine is the action itself, and the reward might be a quick "Nice job!" fist pump or a checkmark on your tracker. The more you repeat this loop, the more your brain wires it in until you're doing it on autopilot, like putting on pants before leaving the house (hopefully).

If big habits sound intimidating, shrink them down until they're laughably easy. The "tiny habits" approach builds momentum without requiring heroic effort. Want to write a book? Commit to one sentence daily—seriously, just one. Most days you'll write more but setting the bar low beats staring at a blank page. Need to declutter? Try a five-minute "power clean" after dinner—set a timer and race yourself. Meditate before meetings? Two minutes of breathing counts. These micro-habits are like appetizers for bigger changes; they trick your brain into showing up.

To help you brainstorm, here's a quick menu of tiny habits that can fit into almost any schedule: After pouring your morning drink, read one page of something inspiring. After putting on shoes, step outside and take three deep breaths. After logging into work or school, write your top priority on a sticky note. After dinner, set out your workout clothes for tomorrow. After turning off your alarm, list one thing you're grateful for. String a few together and suddenly you have a routine that runs itself.

Now, let's get real habits sometimes break down. Maybe you catch a cold and skip your walk, or finals week flattens your writing streak. That's normal. What matters is how quickly you get back on track. There's a rule I love: "Never miss twice." If you miss a habit once, treat it as a blip, not a failure. Miss it twice in a row? That's your cue to reset before things slide further. Give yourself permission to start small again if needed—remember, progress isn't erased by one skipped day.

Tracking helps too. Visual cues are powerful motivators because they let you see streaks grow—and no one wants to break a winning chain. Try using an app like Habitica or Streaks to gamify your habits (Calm, 2023) or go old-school with a paper tracker taped to your fridge or desk. Each checkmark is proof you showed up for yourself, however briefly.

If motivation dips and old routines creep back in, troubleshoot instead of judging yourself. Ask: Was my cue obvious enough? Was my reward satisfying? Did I try to change too much at once? Sometimes life just gets wild—so shrink the habit until it fits again. If meditating for ten minutes feels impossible, drop it to sixty seconds while things are hectic.

If you want an extra nudge, pair habits with social rewards—text a friend when you complete your tiny action, snap a photo of your post-clean desk, or share your streaks online if that fuels you. Just keep it playful and personal; comparison drains energy faster than a phone with twenty apps running at once.

Eventually, these habits become as natural as tying your shoes or scrolling through memes before bed (hey, I see you). The point isn't perfection—it's consistency over time. Even when motivation wobbles or life gets weird, these small actions stack up until change feels effortless and automatic.

THE "ENERGY AUDIT"—MAXIMIZING YOUR BEST HOURS

So, here's a truth nobody tells you when you're setting big goals: your energy is not a steady, reliable faucet. It's more like a mischievous cat —sometimes curled up and purring, other times hiding where you least expect. If you've ever started a project full of energy in the morning, only to stare blankly at your screen by 2 p.m., you know what I mean. Everyone has natural rhythms, and the secret sauce to real progress is matching your goal work to those peaks. Forget "rise and grind" or "just power through." Let's talk about learning when your brain and body are ready to shine.

Begin with an energy audit. For one week, keep an energy log. Start when you wake up and rate your energy each hour on a scale of 1 to 10. Don't overthink it—just jot a number in a notebook, on your phone, or even sticky notes. Note what you're doing: Are you groggy at 9 a.m., peaking at 11, then crashing after lunch? Do you get a mysterious second wind at 8 p.m.? You might notice you're a morning "lark," an evening "owl," or somewhere in between. This data is gold. Maybe afternoons are your productivity kryptonite, or perhaps your creativity blooms after dinner. Everyone's pattern is unique, so don't judge—just observe.

Once you've got your numbers, look for patterns. That mid-morning spike? That's prime real estate for your most important work—

creative writing, deep problem-solving, or anything that demands focus and originality. Save the low-energy slots (say, the dreaded post-lunch slump) for automatic tasks: clearing email, filling out forms, or reorganizing files. If you have flexibility, block these high-energy windows on your calendar for your biggest goals. Don't let meetings or random requests take over—protect those hours like they're tickets to a sold-out concert.

Here's where delegation and automation become your best friends. If you find yourself running on fumes at certain times, resist the urge to push through with brute force. Is there a report that could be auto generated? Can a teammate handle that low-stakes errand? Can you set up reminders, so you don't have to mentally juggle everything? Use your best brainpower for what truly matters; let technology and teamwork mop up the rest.

Now, not every day cooperates. Sometimes life throws curveballs—a surprise deadline, sick kids, or just plain exhaustion. On these days, energy boosts help. Movement is the quickest fix: a brisk 10-minute walk after lunch can wake up both body and mind. Try standing while working if you feel that late-day sluggishness creeping in—a standing desk or even perching at your kitchen counter does wonders for circulation and alertness. Nutrition counts too. Swap heavy, carb-laden lunches for something lighter and protein-rich if possible; nobody does their best thinking after a giant burrito-induced food coma.

Environment tweaks can also shift the energy equation. Open a window for fresh air, play music that makes you want to move, or adjust the lighting if your workspace feels cave-like. Even a quick stretch or splash of cold water on your face can be surprisingly effective when fatigue sets in.

Don't treat your energy audit as a one-and-done event. Life changes—new jobs, school schedules, seasons, and daylight-saving time all mess with our rhythms. Make it a habit to reassess every few months. Set quarterly reminders: "Hey self, how's my energy these days?" If you've changed shifts at work or started night classes, repeat your log for another week and see what's different. Sometimes, just acknowledging that your old routines don't fit anymore is the nudge needed to rework your schedule.

If you want to get geeky (and why not?), use color-coded charts or apps to visualize your patterns over time. You'll spot trends: maybe winter mornings hit different, or maybe summer evenings are pure magic for brainstorming. The point is to stop fighting your natural cycles and start working with them. Treating your energy like the valuable resource it is leads to more progress with less frustration—and frees up willpower for actual decision-making rather than endless self-nagging.

If you share space with roommates, family, or coworkers who don't respect "prime time," communicate your needs directly. Simple statements like "I'm really focused from 9 to 11—can we chat after?" usually do the trick (or at least cut down the interruptions). And if you're in charge of others' schedules, try aligning group work with everyone's best hours whenever possible people will thank you later.

Every person's energy map is different, but everyone benefits from understanding their own peaks and valleys. The more you track and tweak, the easier it gets to work smart instead of just working hard. And if all else fails, remember coffee is great, but knowing yourself is better.

ACCOUNTABILITY THAT STICKS—CHOOSING THE RIGHT PARTNER OR SYSTEM

Accountability acts like the training wheels of progress, offering that extra push to keep you going—especially when motivation starts to fade. Research shows that sharing your goals and progress with others significantly increases your chances of following through. It's not about public shame; rather, it's the small bursts of positive pressure and the shift from private intentions to shared goals. You're much less likely to procrastinate when you know someone—a friend, mentor, or group—will be checking in on your progress.

Accountability can take many forms, so choose what fits you best. Some people work well with an accountability partner—perhaps a friend with parallel ambitions. Regular check-ins could be as simple as a Monday morning "What's your plan?" text. Others prefer a mentor who provides advice and encouragement, not just oversight. Group settings appeal to those who thrive in a social environment, such as mastermind circles, online challenges, or Slack channels for sharing wins and setbacks. Tech-savvy or introverted types might turn to digital tools: apps with social features for logging results and supporting peers, even anonymously.

Tailor your accountability approach to your preferences. If phone calls intimidate you, stick to messaging. Structure lovers might set fixed appointments with a focused format, like weekly top three action lists. If flexibility suits you, keep it casual with voice notes or memes. The goal is a rhythm that matches your life, with the level and style of feedback you genuinely need.

Starting an accountability partnership is simple and doesn't need to be awkward. Set up a clear agreement or "accountability contract." For example: "We'll check in every Friday at 5 p.m. by phone for 15 minutes. Each week, we'll cover: What did I accomplish? What's next? What obstacles came up?" Whether by text or video, clarity upfront helps. Use a simple first message: "Want to be accountability buddies for our goals this month? We could swap weekly updates—a quick 'here's what went well and what's next' check-in." Agree on ground rules, like how candid feedback should be. Decide if you want gentle encouragement, tough love, or a mix—being clear here prevents problems later.

If joining a group, choose one that matches your style. Some groups celebrate wins and publicly highlight missed goals; others emphasize support and idea-sharing. Experiment before committing, and don't hesitate to switch if it's not working. For digital setups, use apps that let you create private teams or community streaks, letting you update progress with people you trust—or just those working on similar goals.

Not every accountability setup will work perfectly. Partners can become unreliable, scheduling can slip, or initial enthusiasm might burn out. If your partner misses several check-ins ("three strikes"), reset expectations or try a new system. Don't take it personally; life gets in the way. Sometimes, solo accountability is better, especially during busy or stressful periods. Create your own rituals—write weekly progress reports to yourself, use sticky notes as reminders, or send scheduled calendar invites to keep yourself on track.

For those wanting a reliable plan, here's a quick accountability contract you can adapt:

Accountability Contract

- Partner(s): _____
- Check-in day/time: _____
- Format (text/call/video/app): _____
- Questions: 1) What did I complete? 2) What's next? 3) Where did I struggle?
- Feedback style: __ Gentle / __ Honest / __ Tough Love
- "Three strikes" policy (missed check-ins): _____

Helpful check-in questions keep things focused:

- "What win are you celebrating this week?"
- "What tripped you up?"
- "What one thing will you tackle before our next check-in?"

If your system stops working—whether your partner drops out, the group falls apart, or the app feels uninspiring—don't give up on accountability. Try new partners, reset rules, or go solo until you find what works. Consistency matters more than perfection. Finding the right structure may take testing different methods, but honest check-ins—whether with others or just yourself—keep your goals within reach.

TACKLING BURNOUT—RECOGNIZING AND RECOVERING BEFORE IT'S TOO LATE

If you've ever wondered whether you're just tired or burned out, you're not alone. Burnout goes way beyond needing a nap or feeling "meh" about your to-do list. It's a sneaky, slow-building storm that starts with fatigue and ends with you dreading even the smallest tasks. Unlike a bad day, burnout isn't fixed by a single good night's sleep or a fun weekend. It's emotional exhaustion that sticks around, making you cynical, irritable, and convinced nothing you do matters. Your brain feels foggy. Your patience gets thin as dental floss. Even things you once enjoyed seeming dull. Burnout is the moment you look at your goal and think, "Why bother?"

Spotting burnout early is a superpower. Most people ignore the warning signs until they're knee-deep in stress soup. You don't have to wait until you're snapping at your cat for breathing too loudly. Try this quick checklist: Are you dreading your goal-related work? Do you feel detached, like a robot on autopilot? Have you noticed your motivation evaporate, replaced by sarcasm or numbness? Are simple mistakes multiplying, or does every task feel like climbing Everest in flip-flops? If yes pops up more than once, pause and take a self-inventory. Burnout often masks itself as "just being busy" or "normal stress," but it's really your mind waving a red flag.

Let's talk strategy—because waiting to "tough it out" just makes things worse. First up: rest, and I mean real rest. Not scrolling social media until your eyeballs hurt or pretending that folding laundry counts as self-care. If you're deep in the warning zone, schedule a full day off from your goal work. Guilt-free. You might be surprised how hard this feels if you're used to hustling non-stop, but it's non-negotiable for recovery. If a full day feels impossible, try micro-breaks: step away for ten minutes every hour, stretch, hydrate, and reset your breathing. Don't underestimate the power of stepping outside for even five minutes—a change in scenery can work wonders.

Sometimes, what your brain needs most is a "digital Sabbath." No screens after dinner—no doomscrolling, no email-checking—just something analog like reading, drawing, or hanging out with real people (or pets). Screens keep your mind buzzing long after you think you've shut down for the night. Another quick fix: practice deep breathing or listen to a short, guided meditation. Even two minutes can lower stress hormones and help your mind reboot.

Recovery is only half the battle—prevention is where you regain control. Set up what I call "burnout boundaries." These are regular check-ins where you ask yourself tough questions: Am I still enjoying this? Does my motivation feel steady or shaky? Am I snapping at people more than usual? Put a monthly self-check on your calendar— make it as routine as paying bills or washing your sheets (hopefully more often than the latter). During these check-ins, rate your stress on a scale from 1 to 10 and notice any creeping cynicism or dread.

Building self-care rituals into your routine can keep burnout at bay. This could be as simple as protecting one evening each week for downtime—no chores, no goal talk, just something that refuels you. If you like structure, create a "burnout safety plan." List your warning signs—maybe you get headaches, start skipping meals, or lose interest in hobbies—and the first actions to take when they appear. For example: "If I dread my project three days in a row, I will take a half-day break and call a friend." This isn't weakness—it's wise maintenance.

Flexibility with timelines helps too. If life throws chaos your way and progress stalls, adjust your goals without beating yourself up. Perfectionism feeds burnout: adaptability prevents it. Remember, progress sometimes means slowing down so that you don't stop altogether.

Burnout isn't just for high-powered executives or overworked students—it can creep up on anyone with ambition and drive. The real secret is noticing it early and responding with kindness toward yourself instead of pushing harder out of habit or guilt. Catching burnout before it blooms keeps your motivation intact and makes it possible to finish strong instead of fizzling out.

Wrapping up this chapter on motivation: remember it's not all about pushing forward. Sometimes it means pulling back just enough to recharge. Energy, habits, and enthusiasm are all renewable resources if you treat them with care. Up next: we'll explore how to track progress meaningfully and adjust course as life changes—because finishing well is about more than just starting strong.

Don't get buried in busy. Use tools that work for you, not ones that steal your time.

— VALARIE V. HENRY

7

TIME, TOOLS, AND TACTICS— FITTING GOALS INTO A BUSY LIFE

TIME-BLOCKING FOR REAL PEOPLE—DESIGNING YOUR "NON-NEGOTIABLE" WINDOWS

If you ever look at your week and think only a clone could fit in your goals and still sleep, you're not alone. Wearing many hats makes time seem to disappear fast. But most people don't need more hours—just better boundaries around their time. This is where time-blocking can make all the difference, helping you move the needle on your goals without becoming a productivity robot.

Forget that time-blocking means color-coding every minute into a rigid, stressful grid. The real (and practical) version is flexible and forgiving, made for leaders, parents, students, and anyone whose carefully laid plans get regularly hijacked by urgent emails, surprise meetings, or needy pets. Real-world time-blocking is more like sketching your week in pencil than etching it in stone—it's adaptive, with plenty of eraser room for life's curveballs.

Here's how to start: pick your "non-negotiable windows"—the minimum, realistic blocks of time you can commit to your main goal. It's not your dream schedule, but what's doable. Maybe it's two 30-minute slots before breakfast each week, Sunday afternoons, or one evening with your phone on silent and door closed. The point isn't to find lots and lots of time but to be consistent with whatever you can set aside reliably. Even a protected hour makes a difference week after week. Guard this time. It's your sacred window for progress.

To visualize this, sketch a grid with days as columns and times (morning, afternoon, evening) as rows. Fill in work (blue), family or school (yellow), your goal windows (green), and downtime (gray). Add white spaces for "buffer zones"—your shock absorbers for chaos, emergencies, or spontaneous ice cream outings. If you prefer digital tools, use your calendar app. Set recurring events labeled "Goal Sprint," color them boldly, and make them prominent—so they don't get trampled by dentist appointments or routine meetings.

Here's an example layout:

Sample Weekly Time Grid

Time	Monday	Tuesday	Wednesday	Thursday	Friday	Saturday	Sunday
Morning	Work	Work	Work	Work	Work	Buffer	Buffer
Afternoon	Work	Work	Work	Work	Work	Family/School	Downtime
Evening	Goal Time	Goal Time	Family/School	Goal Time	Goal Time	Downtime	Downtime

Color Legend:

Work	
Family/School	
Goal Time	
Downtime	
Buffer	

No need for fancy apps or design skills—even a rough hand-drawn version does the job.

Of course, schedules sometimes explode. Your Tuesday morning block might get ambushed by urgent work or a minor meltdown. Here's where flexibility matters: instead of erasing everything, reschedule. Move that block to Thursday lunch or squeeze it on Friday after work. And if your week turns upside down, go smaller—try "micro-blocking," fitting in 10–15 minutes here and there. Over time, those small pockets add up: maybe you jot down a quick project outline in one burst and draft an email in another.

Don't fall into the all-or-nothing trap. Miss a block? It's not game over. Just nudge it forward and keep moving. Consistent effort—showing up often—matters more than never making a mistake. No guilt trips, just a quick pivot and carry on. As long as you keep protecting some goal time, it pays off.

Interactive Element: Weekly Block Mapping Exercise

Grab a notebook or open your favorite calendar app. First, shade your non-negotiable commitments (work, classes, family). Highlight at least two "non-negotiable" slots for your goal, no matter how small. Add buffer zones (empty blocks). Then, plan B: write, "If my main block is lost, I'll swap in _____ as my backup." Keep this grid visible and update it as needed throughout the week.

Flexible time-blocking won't magically add hours to your life—but it does turn scattered minutes into tangible progress. Over time, you'll get good at defending your goal time, and those small blocks will generate real, lasting results.

THE DIGITAL TOOLKIT—APPS AND TEMPLATES FOR TRACKING PROGRESS

You're not alone if your goal tracking is a mess of sticky notes, scattered notebooks, or forgotten apps. Using technology to track your progress can save time and mental effort, but you only need one or two reliable digital tools. Choose the ones that genuinely fit your style, avoiding the temptation to collect endless productivity apps. The right digital helpers should make it easier to focus on your goals, not harder.

First, let's cut through the noise. Todo's stands out for its simplicity, cross-device syncing, and smart reminders. You can add tasks like "Finish Chapter 7 by Friday," and it sorts them by date automatically. Need more flexibility? The notion is an all-in-one workspace where you can build goal boards, embed checklists, and create habit trackers —all on one dashboard. It might look complex initially, but starting with a basic template can keep your projects organized.

If you prefer visual tracking habits, Google Sheets is a classic choice for creating straightforward trackers or dashboards to see your progress briefly. Trello is excellent for managing projects, using drag-and-drop boards to show your movement from "to-do" to "done." Each card can contain checklists, notes, and even motivating GIFs— because tracking progress should feel fun.

The main advantage of digital tools is convenience. Apps remind you about upcoming tasks, automate recurring ones, and sync seamlessly across your devices, making it easy to start an idea on your phone and finish it on your computer. Visual dashboards, color-coded tags, and charts help you spot priorities quickly urgent tasks in red, steady progress in green, and items that need attention in yellow. Push notifications keep you on track, acting like a persistent coach (regardless of what you're wearing).

Before you end up overwhelmed by testing every app or perfecting color codes, remember that less is more. Pick one tool for tracking (like Todo's or Notion) and one for reminders (like Google Calendar or your phone's alarm). Use just these for thirty days before trying anything new. Constantly switching apps can kill momentum and leave you feeling scattered. Review what worked for you at the end of the month—were you satisfied with tracking your progress? Did reminders keep you focused or add noise? If a tool isn't working after a fair trial, then (and only then) consider trying another.

My rule is that if I spend more time adjusting my tracking system than working, it's time to simplify. The best app quietly supports your progress without adding complexity. One practical tip: create a one-page digital dashboard with today's tasks, this week's focus, and a quick overview of your progress. If you enjoy writing by hand, snap a photo of your notes and upload them to your chosen app for easy digital backup.

For an extra nudge, invite a friend or accountability buddy to share access to your board or tracker—watching someone else track their wins can motivate you, too. Don't let technology add stress; let it handle reminders and organization, freeing you to focus on real progress.

Above all, use your digital toolkit consistently, not ideally. Set notifications that work for your routine and build a small ritual—perhaps reviewing your dashboard with Sunday coffee. Adjust your setup as your needs shift. The point is to let digital tools energize your progress and keep you organized, not overwhelmed. Stick with what works, and watch your steady wins add up.

CALENDAR CONFIDENCE—TURNING INTENTIONS INTO SCHEDULED ACTIONS

If there's one tool that quietly rules modern life, it's the humble calendar. Yet, for many, the calendar is more like a graveyard for good intentions—a place where dreams go to get double-booked, ignored, or steamrolled by meetings and dental cleanings. Your calendar can work for you, not against you if you treat it as a living, breathing contract with yourself. Instead of using it as a dumping ground for vague "someday" plans, you can turn your calendar into a launchpad that transforms your goals into tangible, scheduled actions.

This approach begins by treating your goal blocks with the same respect as a root canal or an important interview. If you wouldn't casually cancel on your dentist, why bail on your own ambitions? It's time to shift your mindset: "Goal time" isn't extra—it's a real appointment. If you block off Saturday at 10am to "write a proposal," write it in your planner, type it in your phone, and set an alert. When that block appears, show up as if someone else is waiting for you—because Future You is counting on Present You to keep that promise.

One trick to make this stick is color-coding. Assign each category of activity its own shade—maybe green for goal work (because you want it to grow), blue for self-care (calm and restorative), and red for those can't-miss obligations (like meetings or actual emergencies). Seeing a bright pop of green on your week signals where your ambitions get attention, while red reminds you of fixed commitments that aren't optional. Spreading out these colors helps avoid overwhelm and gives you a visual sense of balance. If your week looks like a red tide, it's time to negotiate for greener—because burnout isn't a badge of honor.

Now, let's talk about recurring events. Don't just wish for consistency; schedule it. Make "goal project" time repeat weekly, biweekly, or whatever rhythm fits your reality. Even if life gets wild, having those placeholders makes it easier to defend your time and to reschedule if needed. And don't forget transitions: add a 15-minute buffer before and after deep work blocks. Use that space to switch gears, grab a snack, or breathe. Buffers help prevent the classic "back-to-back burnout" from packing your calendar tighter than a clown car.

Of course, calendars can get cluttered—fast. Ever opened yours and felt like you were staring into the Matrix? When every square is crammed with overlapping reminders, little icons, and cryptic abbreviations, your brain checks out before you start. The fix? Declutter ruthlessly. Once every couple of weeks, scan your calendar for ghost events—recurring meetings you never attend, reminders that no longer serve you, or obligations that make you sigh aloud. Hit delete without remorse. Prioritize appointments that move you closer to your goals or genuinely matter.

Now, about that sinking feeling when you miss a block—goal block, guilt strikes everyone at some point. Maybe you planned to work on your side project Thursday night but ended up wrangling kids or fighting off a headache instead. The temptation is to throw up your hands and write off the week as a failure. Don't fall for that trap. Instead, treat each block as an experiment: if something derails your plan, reschedule it with zero guilt attached. Move it forward a day or slide it into another open spot later in the week. Flexibility beats rigidity every time, and progress over perfection always wins.

You can also use your calendar as a feedback tool. At the end of each week, do a quick review: What blocks worked? Which ones got bumped or ignored? Was there a specific time of day when you kept getting interrupted? Use this information to tweak your schedule for next week—maybe you'll discover Tuesday evenings are useless for focus, but Saturday mornings are golden. Adjust; accordingly, a good calendar evolves with you.

If paper calendars make you feel nostalgic (or give you sticker shock at the bookstore), use them! Some folks thrive on crossing things out with pens and seeing their month spread across the fridge door. Others prefer digital apps with alerts that buzz like an overeager coach. The format doesn't matter; the commitment does.

You may find it motivating to add "celebration" events after big goal blocks—a coffee break after finishing edits, a walk after sending an important email. This reinforces positive habits and gives your brain something fun to anticipate once the work is done.

In short, treat your calendar like an ally, not an adversary. Give your goals the same weight as anything else in your life that matters. With color-coding, recurring appointments, intentional buffers, and regular decluttering, your calendar becomes more than just a place to jot down meetings—it becomes your map to making progress tangible and visible. And when those inevitable hiccups happen (because life is unpredictable), don't punish yourself—adjust and carry on. Consistency, not perfection, is what turns intentions into actual results.

SAYING "NO" WITHOUT GUILT—MAKING ROOM FOR WHAT MATTERS MOST

You know the feeling: another text pops up—"Can you take this on?" or "Want to help with this project?"—and your stomach tightens. You're already juggling too much, but the urge to be helpful, liked, or not "the difficult one" is strong. Even when your plate is overflowing, saying yes feels easier than risking disappointment or awkwardness. Every "yes" you give to something that doesn't match your priorities steals time from the things you want to finish. It's like watering weeds instead of your garden and then wondering why nothing blooms.

Learning to say no is a superpower that nobody teaches in school, but it's necessary to get real traction on your goals. The skill isn't just about refusing requests; it's about doing so without guilt or burning bridges. Start by recognizing the scenarios that most often pull you into unwanted commitments. Maybe it's the group chat where someone always needs a volunteer, the co-worker who assumes you'll cover their shift again, or even those recurring family "emergencies" that somehow land in your lap. Identify these traps before you're caught off guard, and you'll cut your stress in half.

One trick I've found helpful is crafting default "no" responses ahead of time. Having these scripts ready means, you won't freeze when put on the spot. For example, if someone asks for help with a weeknight event during a crunch period, you can say, "I appreciate you thinking of me, but I'm protecting my evenings for a project right now." Or if you're asked to join another committee or take on more work: "Thanks for asking, but I'm at capacity this month and need to stay focused." These aren't excuses—they're honest boundaries. If you want an easy default, try this: "Let me check my schedule and get back to you." This pause allows you to review your priorities before agreeing to anything new.

It helps to rehearse these phrases out loud, so they come naturally when needed. Stand in front of the mirror or practice with a friend. Your version might sound more casual—"Not this time, but thanks!"— or more formal: "That's a great opportunity, but I'm committed else-where right now." The key is to make your response sound like you, not a robot reading from a manual. If you're worried about hurting someone's feelings, remember that people respect honesty more than empty promises or half-hearted efforts.

Often, the pressure to say yes is rooted in wanting to be liked or feeling responsible for everyone else's happiness. But giving away your time leaves less for what lights you up. Psychologically, setting limits isn't selfish—it's healthy for everyone involved. When you put your priorities first, others learn it's possible and healthy to do the same. You also model boundaries that give others permission to protect their own schedules. It's like being the first person at a party brave enough to dance; suddenly, everyone else feels free to join in.

Defaulting to yes leaves no space for what matters most. If you always say yes to every invitation, extra shift, or "quick favor," your goals become invisible buried under a mountain of obligations that don't even belong to you. This isn't just bad for productivity; it leads to resentment and burnout. When you say no with clarity and respect, people may be disappointed briefly, but most will understand—and many will secretly wish they had your resolve.

Anticipating tricky situations helps, too. Before busy seasons or big deadlines, decide which types of requests are automatic nos. For example, you might choose not to take on new weeknight commitments during a major project sprint. If asked to volunteer or attend another event, your default is: "I'm heads-down on something important right now and can't add anything new." No need to over-explain —clarity is kindness.

As you get used to saying no without apology, pay attention to how your energy changes. Do you feel lighter? Less stretched? More focused? That's your signal that you're making space for what matters most—your goals and well-being. Saying no isn't a failure; it's a decision to put yourself and your vision on the list for once.

Challenge yourself: Write down three default "no" phrases right now. Practice them until they roll off your tongue naturally. The next time someone asks for more than you can give, use one confidently and watch what happens. People will likely respect your honesty, and your schedule will thank you, too.

PROGRESS ON THE GO—GOAL-SETTING TACTICS FOR LIFE IN MOTION

Life rarely unfolds in neat, uninterrupted blocks of time. If you've ever tried to finish a big project but found yourself answering emails in a doctor's waiting room instead of half-listening to a podcast while stuck in traffic, you'll know how fast "free time" can vanish. The good news? You don't need perfect conditions or an empty calendar to make progress. Real life happens on the move—so your goals should move with you.

Mobility is your secret weapon. Think of your commutes, walks, and those odd five-minute lulls as hidden pockets of potential. You can use simple tactics to squeeze value from moments that most people write off. For example, recording voice memos during a drive transforms windshield time into a brainstorming session. Got ideas for your next project? Dictate them, rambling and rough, into your phone's recorder—you can organize them later, but the spark is captured before it fades. Similarly, if you're riding public transit or waiting for a friend who's always late, queue up podcasts or audiobooks that fuel your goal. You can learn on the fly, whether it's leadership lessons, language practice, or that "how to pitch" story you keep meaning to read.

Breaking big tasks into "portable" mini goals turns idle minutes into productive wins. Instead of aiming to write an entire report in one sitting, pull out your phone and draft a quick outline while grabbing lunch solo. Jot down three bullet points for tomorrow's meeting in a note app while waiting for your coffee. Review a one-page worksheet on your tablet as you stay at the dentist. When you think in small, self-contained chunks, you lower the barrier to getting started—no giant mental leap required. It's like carrying around mental trail mix: easy to snack on whenever you get hungry for progress.

One of my favorite tricks is keeping a "Grab and Go" kit. Mine usually includes a beat-up notebook, an extra pen (because pens have an annoying habit of disappearing), and my tablet loaded with whatever I'm working on—a goal worksheet, outline, or reading material. Preload your phone with editable docs or cloud-based tools if you're more digitally inclined. In your note's app, you might keep inspirational quotes, templates, or even mind maps handy. The idea is simple: when life hands you a pocket of time, you're ready to pounce instead of scrolling aimlessly through social media.

Creating anchor activities helps cement these micro-moments into habits. For example, whenever I board a bus or train, I automatically review my top three goals for the week. During daily walks—outside or on a treadmill—I reflect on what's working and needs adjusting. These routines become second nature with repetition, turning forgettable moments into mini check-ins or brainstorming bursts.

To make these tactics stick, tailor them to your lifestyle and preferences. If you love music, create playlists that boost focus or spark creativity during walks or drives. If you're prone to distraction (who isn't?), set up gentle reminders—like a sticky note on your dashboard saying "Voice Memo?" or a calendar alert before lunch prompting you to check your progress. The key is not perfection but presence: being ready to catch those fleeting moments and put them to use.

Of course, there are days when even five minutes feels like a luxury. On those days, celebrate a tiny win anyway—maybe just reviewing your goal list or reading one page from an inspiring book count as progress. Over time, these micro-wins stack up into something substantial. You'll be surprised at how much you can accomplish by chipping away at big goals during life's "in-between" times.

What's powerful about mobile goal tactics is their adaptability. They fit around soccer practices, shift work, or unpredictable schedules. You don't have to wait for the stars to align or the house to be silent. You need the willingness to squeeze value from whatever time and tools you have.

Wrapping this chapter: remember that progress is not always about grand gestures or perfect plans—it's about persistence and creativity in real life's messiness. Whether at home, in transit, or squeezing in five minutes between calls, you've got everything you need to keep moving forward. Next, we'll dig into how to track progress and adjust your approach—so that every effort counts and every step brings you closer to absolute victory.

The measure of intelligence is the ability to change.

— ALBERT EINSTEIN

8

PROGRESS TRACKING— MAKING SUCCESS VISIBLE AND ADJUSTING ON THE FLY

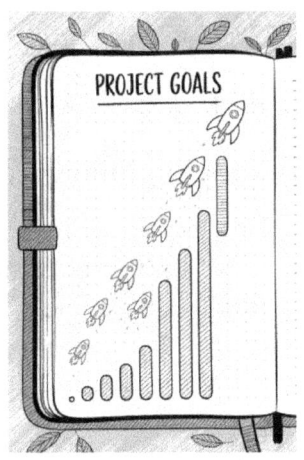

THE CUSTOMIZABLE PROGRESS TRACKER—VISUALIZING RESULTS YOUR WAY

People love visible change—before-and-after shots, makeovers, and other tangible signs of forward movement. Our brains crave proof of getting somewhere, not just vague ideas. Yet, with personal goals, progress can be invisible, quietly accumulating until we overlook how much ground we've covered. That's why tracking is more than a suggestion; it's the tool that turns dreams into reality. But progress tracking doesn't have to be rigid or overwhelming; it should match your life, personality, and habits.

Some people love digital dashboards, complete with color-coded charts and reminders. With each small win, others get absolute satisfaction from peeling off a sticker or doodling in a journal. The key is finding or creating a method you'll use, not one you'll abandon because it feels like a chore. Be flexible—switch things up if needed. Start a bullet journal or use wall charts for visual checkmarks if you prefer analog. If digital tools excite you, test out goal-tracking apps (free and paid abound—avoid collecting apps just for novelty). Spreadsheet lovers can use Google Sheets for milestone charts and fun color-coded progress bars. Visual thinkers might enjoy posters, like a classic fundraising thermometer, filling up as you reach your target.

Let's get practical. Suppose your goal is 10,000 steps a day for a month: add a gold star on your wall calendar for every day you hit your goal, forming a constellation of wins. If you're writing a short story, use different colors to cross off each finished section in your journal. Make a spreadsheet and color for professional certifications in each stage you complete—watch it fill up like a victory parade. Raising money? Use a poster thermometer; update the shading as pledges arrive and put it somewhere you'll see daily for constant motivation and accountability.

Visibility is important. Trackers work best where you'll notice them regularly—not hidden away or buried in an app. Place yours on the fridge, by your desk, on your mirror, or use it as your phone wallpaper. The more visible it is, the more you'll remember to update it and the prouder you'll feel as it fills up. This isn't about bragging (unless you want to)—it's about showing yourself that every step matters. Quick glances at those checkmarks or trend lines provide a powerful motivation boost, especially on tough days.

Consistency matters more than perfection. Updating your tracker should become a habit—after breakfast, before bed, or linked to another routine. Some people review their tracker weekly, admiring filled-in squares and reflecting on their habits. Did you do better on certain days? Did weekends lead to progress or pause? These observations aren't for self-criticism but to provide helpful feedback. At the end of the month, explore "trend spotting." Look for what helped during high points and what caused slowdowns or setbacks.

Interactive Element: Build-Your-Own Progress Tracker Exercise

1. Choose Your Style: Choose from analog options (journal, stickers, chart) or Digital options (app, spreadsheet, dashboard).
2. Decide on Visuals: Pick colors, shapes, or symbols that appeal to you.
3. Choose Placement: List three obvious spots you'll see every day.
4. Set Update Ritual: Decide when to update—daily or weekly, ideally tied to another habit.
5. Reflect Every Month: Use prompts—
   ○ What patterns do I see?
   ○ Which days or weeks were easier? Why?
   ○ When did I need extra support or a more flexible approach?

Tracking progress should motivate, not feel like a burden. If you start dreading it, change your system: swap digital for analog, use new visuals, or get an accountability buddy. The right tracking system is the one you'll continue with, even when life gets messy.

Ultimately, it's about making progress visible in an authentic and rewarding way. Tangible records—on paper, screen, or sticky notes—make your wins harder to ignore and easier to celebrate. When setbacks happen (which they will), these records also remind you that growth is happening, even if every day doesn't feel epic. Make your progress tracker personal and playful if you like, but make sure it's yours.

WEEKLY WINS REVIEW—CELEBRATING SUCCESSES, LARGE AND SMALL

Most people struggle to give themselves credit. By Friday, you may only recall the stress, the missed calls, or the unfinished task, overlooking a week's worth of real progress, big or small. That's why a Weekly Wins Review isn't just meaningless fluff; it's your personal highlight reel. Regularly celebrating what went right keeps you motivated, builds resilience, and retrains your mind to notice progress rather than just problems. Positive psychology research (The Psychology Group, n.d.) shows that acknowledging small wins fuels motivation, improves mood, and enhances focus for future challenges. This isn't about collecting trophies—it's about expecting and seeking progress.

A meaningful Weekly Wins Review should be easy and satisfying. Pick a time that works—Sunday evening with tea, Friday after work, or Monday morning. Use prompts that go beyond the obvious. Ask: "What am I proud of this week?" Notice the significant accomplishments and the smaller wins that are easy to miss. "What small win made me smile?" Wins might be hitting a target, skipping doomscrolling, or eating a vegetable. "Where did I show up differently?" Perhaps you spoke up in a meeting after staying quiet for months or finally sent a challenging email—both counts.

Don't just focus on measurable achievements like "completed four workouts" or "finished editing two chapters." Look for qualitative shifts: "I handled criticism better," "I reframed a setback," or "I stayed calm in traffic." These often matter more over time than numbers on a chart. If you're tracking habits, include them: "Meditated three mornings," "kept my phone out of the bedroom," or "chose water over soda (twice)." Any step forward counts.

Sharing your wins can make the review energizing. Make it a ritual for accountability and fun. Review solo, with a partner, or in a group. Some people enjoy Friday "celebration calls" with a friend—swap stories, share proud moments, and celebrate with a virtual high-five.

Online communities thrive on this energy. Posting weekly wins builds momentum for everyone. If you're private, jot them in your planner or send a voice note to yourself.

My step-by-step template for your Weekly Wins Review:

1. Set the scene: Choose your time and space. Make it pleasant—a favorite drink, comfy chair, or playlist.

2. Reflect with prompts:

- What am I proud of this week?
- What small win made me smile?
- Where did I stretch myself?
- What challenge did I handle better?
- What did I learn about myself?

3. List both types of wins:

- Quantitative: concrete steps ("called three clients," "wrote 750 words," "saved $20").
- Qualitative: mindset shifts ("felt more confident in meetings," "let go of perfectionism," "was kinder to me after a mistake").

4. Celebrate:

- Tell someone (text, call, group chat).
- Physically check off or highlight your wins.
- Treat yourself—music, snack, quick victory dance, whatever works.

5. Note what helped:

- Did a specific routine help? Did support matter? Was a new approach practical?

6. Set a mini-intention for next week:

- Carry momentum forward by choosing one small action or mindset to keep.

To boost accountability and energy, make your review social at least monthly—a quick call with a friend, posting in a group, or a five-minute pre-weekend wins share with coworkers. Saying your progress aloud—or typing it—reinforces a growth mindset.

Remember, small wins deserve celebration, too. They stack up into bigger accomplishments over time and recognizing them trains your mind to spot positives instead of gaps. This ritual isn't bragging or pretending things are perfect—it's about honoring effort, resilience, and growth, every awkward or wonderful step on the journey.

If you like, keep a running list of weekly wins in your journal or app and review it monthly. You'll notice moments you'd otherwise forget that moved you closer to your goals. The Weekly Wins Review isn't just another to-do; it's fuel for future progress and proof that you're moving forward, even when it doesn't feel obvious.

THE "REALITY CHECK-IN"—COURSE CORRECTING WITHOUT SHAME

Everyone loves a good plot twist in movies, but surprises aren't always as entertaining regarding our progress. You set out with a plan—maybe even a color-coded one—only to discover that real life has creative ideas. Perhaps you thought a project would take two hours, but it ballooned into six because you forgot how long research takes (or that your dog would need three emergency walks). Here is where the "reality check-in" earns its stripes. This isn't about grilling yourself under a spotlight or assigning blame. It's about taking an honest look at what's working, what's stuck, and what needs to shift—like a friendly GPS recalculating your route after a wrong turn, minus the robotic voice and existential dread.

Normalize these check-ins. They're not confessionals. You're not on trial. Regular, honest assessments are the secret sauce for anyone who's ever felt motivated and overwhelmed by their goals. The reality check-in is your chance to pause and ask: "What progress did I expect?" "What happened?" "What got in the way?" No drama, just facts, and curiosity. You may have planned to finish three chapters of a report but only completed one because the rest of your week exploded with surprise meetings and a cold that knocked you flat. Maybe you aimed to run five miles but hit a wall at two after realizing you ate only cookies for lunch (no judgment—we've all been there).

This isn't about self-judgment but gathering clues and making the next steps smarter. Start with facts: what did you set out to do, and where did the story head off-road? Did you underestimate how challenging a task would be? Did life throw you a curveball, like a family emergency or unexpected work deadline? A compassionate reality check means looking at these detours with curiosity, not criticism. It's like being your own detective—minus the trench coat and magnifying glass—except you're solving for progress, not whodunit.

After you identify what happened, shift to adjustments. Sometimes, you'll realize a timeline was pure fantasy—there's no shame in redrawing the map. Maybe you promised daily gym sessions but forgot that Tuesdays are packed with back-to-back obligations. Pause and ask: "Do I need to give myself more time?" "Would it help to break this goal into smaller pieces?" If life got wild (like your kid needed stitches or your boss dropped a project on your desk at 4:55 pm), acknowledge it. This isn't an excuse; it's context. Sometimes, the best move is to revise your plan, extend deadlines, or even put a goal on ice for now.

And do not be afraid to swap goals if something bigger or more urgent pops up. Imagine you set out to write every morning, but halfway through the month, you get accepted into a leadership program that demands extra time and focus. It's okay—no one gets a medal for stubbornly clinging to the old plan when new opportunities or realities demand change. Adaptation is not quitting; it's proof that you're paying attention.

When things stall, document what you learn for next time. Did you underestimate how long a task would take? Write, "Next time, schedule double the buffer before deadlines." Did your initial approach flop? Instead of sulking (tempting as that may be), jot down, "This strategy didn't work—what other methods can I experiment with?" Maybe you discover that working in sprints suits you better than marathon sessions. Or perhaps late nights kill your focus, but mornings give you superpowers.

Over time, these notes become your personal playbook for growth. Patterns will emerge certain times of year are always chaotic, or maybe you're consistently optimistic about how much you can squeeze into a single day (join the club). Use these insights not as ammunition for guilt but as fuel for more thoughtful planning.

Here's a practical template for your next check-in:

1. What progress did I expect this week/month?
2. What happened?
3. What factors helped or hindered me?
4. What adjustments do I need—timeline change, new strategy, or different goal?
5. What lesson will I carry forward?

If you ever feel ashamed over a missed target, remember everyone course-corrects. Even Olympic athletes and CEO superstars tweak their plans (sometimes after spectacular flops). Shame belongs nowhere near your plans; what matters is using every twist as feedback for future wins.

The reality check-in proves you're human—a creative, resourceful, sometimes cookie-powered human learning and adapting on the fly. Every honest assessment moves you closer to goals that fit your real life, not just your ideal calendar.

THE REFLECTION PAUSE—BUILDING SELF-AWARENESS THROUGH GUIDED PROMPTS

Some think reflection is what happens when you stare at yourself in a shiny toaster. I see it as something much richer—a purposeful pause where you step out of autopilot, look at what's happening behind your eyes, and notice patterns hiding in plain sight. Intentional reflection is like running a diagnostic on your own operating system. You start to see the not-so-obvious reasons why some days felt electric while others seemed like wading through peanut butter. It's less about navel-gazing and more about detective work, poking around in your choices, reactions, and routines to see what's driving your progress or tripping you up. This isn't just for the philosophers or the overly sentimental; it's for anyone who wants to stop running the same tired laps around the same old track. When you start building regular reflection pauses into your months or quarters, you unlock smarter decisions because you finally understand what works for you—and what's just noise.

I like to make reflection actionable, not abstract. That means using guided prompts—questions that cut through the mental fog and force honest answers. Try these: "What energized me most since my last check-in?" That could be anything from leading a project to a sponta-neous walk that sparked fresh ideas. "What drained me?" Maybe it was endless emails, a toxic group chat, or even self-imposed pressure to be perfect (that's a sneaky one). "Where did I surprise myself?" Perhaps you kept calm during a crisis or picked up an old skill faster than expected. Go deeper: "What belief changed for me this month?" Some-times, you realize you can say no without the world crumbling or that asking for help doesn't mean you're weak.

Don't get boxed in by traditional journaling if it feels stiff. Reflection should suit your style, not the other way around. Some folks pour their thoughts into notebooks, scribbling with reckless abandon until the page contains insight and coffee stains. Others find clarity talking aloud—hit record on your phone and let your thoughts spill out in real-time. People sketch mind maps after big projects, drawing lines between lessons and new ideas like connecting constellations. Creativity counts; you might even mix formats: jot quick notes on paper after a meeting, then record an audio message to yourself after hitting a milestone. If you finish a 30-day goal sprint, try narrating how you felt before and after—notice which parts made you glow, and which made you want to crawl under a blanket and never emerge.

Monthly or quarterly reflection pauses don't have to happen in solitude. Sharing key insights with someone else will multiply the benefits. It forces clarity when you say something aloud to a trusted friend, mentor, or even your cat (no judgment). Sometimes, stating, "I realized this month that I do my best thinking outside, away from screens," is enough to cement a new habit. If you're part of a mastermind group or accountability circle—even if it's just a tight group chat —try posting one "Aha!" moment at the end of each month. Watch how the group reacts; often, their feedback will help spot blind spots you never considered.

Reflection can be light or deep, quick or sprawling—what matters is that it's real. Don't just ask what went well or what tanked; look for recurring themes. Are there certain types of tasks that always light you up? Do some environments drain your energy without fail? Is there a belief about yourself that keeps shifting as you stack up more evidence of your growth? The point isn't to psychoanalyze yourself into oblivion but to gather enough self-awareness that your next round of choices is sharper, more aligned, and less likely to end in facepalm moments.

Here's a nudge: once a month, carve out twenty minutes just for reflection—schedule it like you would a non-negotiable meeting with someone important (spoiler: that someone is you). Pick three prompts from above or invent your own. Write, talk, sketch, or even dance it out if that feels honest. Capture what stands out, then revisit those notes before planning your next set of moves. If you notice a pattern, like realizing every time you skip breakfast, your productivity nosedives—write it down and consider how to tweak things next month. And if you hit on something big, don't be shy about sharing; someone else is probably wrestling with the same thing and could use your spark.

In reflection pauses, wisdom sneaks in and whispers, "Hey, here's what matters." These are where all your progress tracking and reality checks finally gel into understanding. You don't have to do them perfectly or turn them into a ritual with candles and chanting (unless you want to). You must make space for honesty, curiosity, and maybe some weirdness—and watch how much clearer your next steps become.

CELEBRATING MILESTONES—HOSTING YOUR OWN "WINS WALL" EVENT

Pausing to say, "Hey, I did that," carries real power. Whether you've finished a big project, maintained a running streak, or meditated for several days, every milestone deserves more than a fleeting acknowledgment. It's not about bragging but recognizing your effort, growth, and progress. Too often, achievements blur as we chase the next goal. Taking time to celebrate—no matter the size—boosts your motivation, gives your brain a sweet shot of dopamine, and helps your wins stick in your memory. Consider it a mental high-five before your next endeavor.

You don't need a parade (unless you want one). The key is to make milestones intentional events—a "Wins Wall" celebration that matches your style. If you prefer solitude, write a note to your future self and save it for later. If community energizes you, host a virtual collage party—gather photos, tokens, or screenshots of your journey and share them with friends on a video call. Prefer in-person moments? Host a small "goal toast" over dinner or coffee, where everyone briefly shares something they're proud of, no matter how small.

There are countless creative ways to honor progress. Once you hit a goal, reward yourself with a treat or a spontaneous day trip. Going public on social media isn't just about attention—it can build motivation and accountability, too. If your friends are far away, try a group

"Wins Wall": everyone posts pictures or notes about their achievements. How you celebrate isn't the point; it's that you make the time to do it.

Grand celebrations combine reflection and anticipation. During your Wins Wall moment, think about your journey: What did you learn? What surprised you? Speak your lesson out loud, even if it's just to your pet—"I learned I can stick with things longer than I thought," or "I reached out when I needed support." Add a symbol, note, or quote to your Wins Wall to make the lesson tangible for your future self.

Don't rush this acknowledgment. These moments rewire your brain for resilience and persistence, reinforcing that big successes result from many small steps. If you feel motivated, set a new intention or goal—write it down, say it aloud, or create a visual cue to remind you what's next.

A favorite ritual is ending a Wins Wall event by adding the next target to your wall—a sticky notes with your next milestone, a postcard representing a future goal, or suggestions from friends for new challenges. Make it interactive if you wish; it's all about building anticipation for future progress.

If you ever feel silly celebrating alone, remember that recognizing your own effort is a leadership trait that nurtures joy and growth. Whether solo or with a group, Wins Wall celebrations tell you that your persistence matters and your journey deserves recognition.

Remember—a milestone celebration doesn't need to be flashy or public to count. It just needs to be meaningful and intentional. Marking your wins locks in your confidence and helps you face the next challenge.

Quick Exercise: Plan Your Next "Wins Wall" Celebration

1. Choose a milestone (big or small).
2. Pick your style: solo reflection, group chat, dinner toast, public post, collage, or another meaningful project.

3. Prepare something concrete: a letter, a small token, a bouquet, or a collage.
4. Take five minutes to reflect on lessons learned.
5. Set one intention or symbol for your next goal—add it to your Wins Wall as new motivation.

Every tracked achievement and celebrated milestone add momentum that makes future goals feel possible—even inevitable. Recognizing your wins isn't just feel-good fluff—it's fuel. As you move forward, remember that progress tracking brings meaning and measurement. Next, we'll explore how to recover from setbacks and keep moving ahead when life gets tough.

You either win or you learn.

— JOHN C. MAXWELL

9

RESILIENCE, RECOVERY, AND REBOUND—HANDLING SETBACKS LIKE A PRO

THE RECOVERY ACTION PLAN—WHAT TO DO WHEN YOU FALL OFF TRACK

No one boasts about failing a 30-day challenge or eating chips for dinner when their meal prep falls apart. Still, everyone—yes, everyone—goes off track at some point. Missed milestones and lost momentum are universal, not signs of failure. Those who seem to "crush it" usually restart more often than most; their advantage is recovering faster and smarter, not giving up or spiraling into blame.

Here's your playbook for handling setbacks. First, pause and acknowledge what happened—no drama required. Did you miss a deadline or skip multiple workouts? Admit it's a blip, not a catastrophe. Don't dwell or dramatize—notice the setback and, if possible, find humor in the situation. Free of self-judgment, this pause lessens the sting and helps you move forward.

Next, assess what went wrong by focusing on facts, not feelings. Approach the situation like a curious detective, not a harsh judge. Discard exaggerated stories ("I always fail!" "I'm just lazy!") and pinpoint what got in the way. Maybe you overscheduled, got hit by unexpected chaos, or made unrealistic plans. Write down the real obstacles and see if there's a pattern. Sometimes, the goal was too ambitious, or life threw an unavoidable curveball.

Then, choose a single, doable next step. Resist the urge to overcompensate with an overwhelming catch-up plan—that rarely works. Instead, pick one action you can take now or tomorrow: reply to one email, take a five-minute walk, or brainstorm a few ideas. The aim is to restart your momentum, not create an epic comeback. Small wins matter, and progress thrives on them—perfectionism does not.

Once you have your next move, let someone in your support circle know—an accountability partner, supportive friend, or your manager if it's work-related. This doesn't require a big confession. Just state what happened and your next action. If you're going solo, write it somewhere you'll see it. Saying the reset out loud or putting it in writing strengthens your commitment.

Here's a quick script you can use:

"I missed my (goal/task) because (reason), so my next step is (action), and I'll check in again on (date)."

Example: "I missed my budgeting check-in because work went late all week, so my next step is to update my expense tracker tonight after dinner, and I'll check in again next Sunday."

Treat resets as regular maintenance, not emergencies. Olympians miss practices. CEOs launch flops. Artists abandon projects. Setbacks aren't a sign of failure—the pros recover, adjust, and keep going. Each comeback builds your resilience and proves you can bounce back.

If setbacks are recurring, don't keep resetting blindly—ask why this pattern keeps happening. Maybe your goals clash with your current life, or there's hidden burnout, stress, or distraction. Sometimes, your mind is stuck on limiting beliefs or unattainable expectations. Start logging your setbacks for a few weeks—you'll likely spot a helpful pattern.

If you stay stuck, look for outside support: a mentor, therapist, or mastermind group (see APA source 25 for ideas). Fresh perspectives often lead to solutions you haven't considered.

Interactive Element: Build Your Recovery Script

Open your notes app or grab a sheet of paper and fill in:

- I missed my _____ because _____, so my next step is _____, and I'll check in again on _____.

Practice with three real-life examples—big or small. Keep this template handy; you'll use it more often than expected.

Ultimately, resilience isn't about never stumbling—it's about getting back on your path quickly and without losing sight of your goal. Each reset increases your flexibility, strength, and chance of eventual success.

REFRAMING FAILURE—TURNING "MISTAKES" INTO VALUABLE DATA

Failure. The word sounds final, dramatic, and embarrassing, like tripping over your shoelaces in front of your boss. But here's a not-so-secret truth: mistakes are baked into the recipe of every success story, no matter how polished the highlight reel looks on Instagram or LinkedIn. High achievers—athletes, business leaders, or artists—don't just stumble more often than you think; they use those stumbles as launchpads. Think about every Olympic medalist who missed a qualifying race, a CEO whose first product tanked, or a writer who wallpapered their room with rejection slips before hitting the big time. Research and anecdotes make it clear: the people who bounce back aren't immune to mistakes; they're just relentlessly treating every setback as feedback, not a verdict. Instead of hiding mistakes in the metaphorical junk drawer, they pull them out, examine them from every angle, and ask, "What can I learn from this mess?"

Picture it: you set an ambitious deadline for a work project or that new side hustle. You tell yourself, "This time, I'll be ahead of schedule!" Fast-forward to the night before—your progress is more "creative procrastination" than "steady advance." The project slips, and you're left with disappointment and maybe a sprinkle of self-criticism. Here's where the magic happens (yes, magic—just minus the rabbits and top hats). Instead of spiraling into "Why am I like this?" territory, pause for a quick debrief. Grab your journal, open a note on your phone, or talk it out with a friend. Start with three questions: What happened? (Stick to the facts—"I underestimated the research time," not "I'm a disaster.") What did I learn? (Maybe you must build buffer days or block social media during work sprints.) What will I try differently next time? (Perhaps set mini-deadlines or ask for help earlier.) This mini "post-mortem" isn't an emotional trial—it's detective work.

Make this a habit if you want to level up your learning. Dedicate a section of your progress journal to "Lessons from my last three setbacks." Write down each fumble: the project that fizzled, the week you bailed on workouts, the speech that didn't land. Under each one, jot down what triggered it and what patterns you notice. Did you overcommit right after a vacation? Did distractions spike after skipping lunch? Chart these recurring themes—you'll spot trends faster than you can say "déjà vu." It's not about shaming yourself; it's about collecting data to outsmart future obstacles. High performers always do this, even if their Instagram captions say #blessed.

Now, let's talk mindset—because how you talk to yourself after a mistake shape what happens next. The trick is to swap judgment for curiosity. Imagine yourself as a scientist in a lab coat (real or imaginary—bonus points for goggles). When a plan flops, try saying, "I'm a scientist, not a judge. This is data, not a verdict." Each mistake is just another experiment with results you can use. If your brain starts drafting mean-spirited internal Yelp reviews ("Would not recommend this performance!"), redirect with questions like: "What experiment can I run next based on what I learned?" or "How might I tweak my process for better results?" These scripts flip the story from failure to innovation.

If you want an interactive boost, here's a worksheet idea: make three columns titled "Mistake," "Trigger," and "Lesson." Fill them in after each setback—no need for fancy charts unless you're into spreadsheets. Over time, this "failure data" collection becomes your playbook. You'll see which triggers trip you up most—maybe it's saying yes too often, skipping sleep before big days, or the siren song of TikTok at 11 p.m. Once those patterns are clear, you can experiment with new strategies instead of repeating old cycles.

The more you treat every misstep as valuable intel instead of evidence against your abilities, the less power mistakes hold over you. This mindset is not just trendy self-help talk; it's supported by research showing that reframing failure as feedback improves resilience and long-term achievement (Farnam Street, 2025). Thomas Edison didn't invent the lightbulb by getting it right the first time—he famously said he found 10,000 ways that didn't work. You don't need 10,000 attempts to succeed at your goals (though if you do hit that number, please write your book), but you need the courage to keep collecting data and trying again.

So next time you spectacularly drop the ball or faceplant, pause, pull on your mental lab coat, and ask what experiment comes next. This is how you build real grit and keep progress moving forward, no matter how messy things get along the way.

THE "PIVOT PROTOCOL" IN ACTION—WHEN AND HOW TO REROUTE

There's a big difference between needing a quick reset, like hopping back on your bike after a bump, and realizing you're headed the wrong way altogether. Sometimes, your goal needs a minor tweak; other times, it requires a complete overhaul. It's easy to get stuck powering through plans that no longer fit. What felt right at the start of the year may now seem as uninspiring as plain oatmeal. So, how do you know if you need a simple reset or a genuine pivot? Start by asking: Am I still a little excited about this goal? Has my situation changed to make my original plan feel wrong, forced, or irrelevant? Do I keep running into the same problems, no matter how many resets I try? Has something shifted in me—my values, interests, or health? If you answer "yes" to more than one, it may be time to reroute, not just reboot.

Deciding when to pivot begins with honest reflection. Ask: What's different now? Maybe there's been a significant life change, like a new job, a baby, a diagnosis, or perhaps the world changed—think layoffs, a pandemic, or realizing your "dream" isn't yours. Next, pinpoint what's not working. Is progress stalled, even with your best efforts? Are you pushing forward with no joy? Or have your priorities shifted, leaving your previous goal at the bottom of your mental list? Then, ask: What feels more right now? Imagine yourself six months from now—what new pursuits energize you?

For example, say you set a marathon goal, but an injury derails running for months. Rather than relinquish exercise or limp in pain, you pivot to "build daily movement." Now, you discover yoga or long walks—shifting from defeat to discovery.

Once you know it's time to pivot, communicate clearly, especially with family, teams, or accountability partners. You don't need a dramatic speech—just honesty and clarity. Try: "I've reflected, and I'm shifting my focus to (new goal) because (reason)." For example: "I'm moving from marathon training to daily mobility because I need to heal and want to be active long term." At work, root your message in shared values: "I believe our energy is better spent on (new direction) because it aligns with our goals." This approach avoids confusion and helps others understand your reasoning.

Pivots should be seen as marks of growth, not signs of quitting. Rerouting means you're adapting. It takes courage to admit what's no longer working and even more to pursue what feels right now. Celebrate your pivot as a win. Share it with your accountability group, post it online if that motivates you, or note the benefits—lower stress, more creativity, improved well-being, and new relationships. These reminders will help on days when doubt creeps in.

Sometimes, the best outcomes follow letting go of the original plan. That "failed" marathon could lead you to discover new activities like climbing or swimming. Shelving a business idea might open doors to partnerships or creative pursuits. Often, new opportunities appear right after a bold pivot. The important thing is to make your own decisions without apology. You're not the same as when you set your old goal, and that's progress. Pivots aren't detours; they're proof you're paying attention and are brave enough to change direction when life changes.

So next time your goal and reality drift apart, pause and work through this protocol: Is it a minor setback or time for a bigger turn? Are your values and actions still aligned? What excites you now? If the answer suggests a new path, reroute without hesitation. Real success comes not from stubbornly clinging to outdated plans but from having the wisdom—and courage—to build new ones when needed. Every thoughtful pivot proves you're not just moving but moving brighter and truer to who you are now.

BUILDING YOUR SUPPORT SQUAD—MASTERMIND GROUPS & COMMUNITY

Trying to get back on track alone after setbacks is tough—it's easy to get stuck, spiral, or give up. That's why superheroes have teams: real-life resilience often comes from your "personal support squad." This isn't just a cheerleading section (though encouragement helps); it's your source for accountability, brainstorming, and that timely "You've got this" text when you're ready to give up.

Let's break down the group. A mastermind group is essentially your board of directors—peers or professionals who meet regularly to tackle challenges, brainstorm, and encourage progress. It isn't top-down coaching; everyone brings their goals and issues to the table. Peer accountability buddies check in more directly (weekly or monthly) to track progress and goals one-on-one. Cheerleader friends may not know your industry, but they're there to pump you up before big moments, send supportive memes, and remind you why you're working so hard. Expert mentors are seasoned guides offering key advice and helping you anticipate challenges. Each type of support meets different needs—sometimes you want tough love, other times gentle encouragement, or simple validation.

Building your squad doesn't require complexity or fanfare. Start by listing people who pursue big goals or honestly care about your growth—friends, colleagues, classmates, online connections, or supportive family. Think about what each person offers: Are they good listeners? Do they challenge and support you? Are they discreet and trustworthy? Pick two to five potential squad mates and send a low-pressure invite: "I'm starting a support group for people serious about their goals—interested in joining?" Arrange a simple first meeting—virtual or in-person—and focus on sharing expectations and preferred frequency.

Set ground rules to keep things smooth and safe. Agree on confiden-tiality, regular check-ins (weekly, biweekly, etc.), preferred format (video, group chat, in-person), and feedback style. For instance, "We're honest but never harsh." Rotating meeting leads keeps things equitable; when someone's busy, they can pass. Use a straightforward agenda: everyone quickly shares a win, a challenge, and their next step —quick, focused, and actionable.

You don't have to build from scratch, either. There are active online forums and Facebook groups for nearly every niche—writers, entrepreneurs, students, fitness, and more. Search for groups that match your goals and values. Lurk is used to gauge the culture—some groups inspire, and others show off. Once comfortable, introduce yourself and share your current goal or obstacle.

As your group gets going, keep check-ins lively and productive. Start each meeting with a "Wins, Challenges, Next Steps" round. When someone's stuck, hold a no-judgment brainstorm where everyone shares one idea. Regularly rotate "spotlight sessions"—a deeper dive where one member gets 15 minutes to discuss a stubborn problem while others listen and suggest solutions. These sessions ensure everyone feels seen and supported.

Celebration is key in any support squad. Celebrate not just significant victories but also comebacks and rebounds. If someone finally gets back on track after a setback or achieves a challenging goal, mark the occasion—a silly gif, meme, or congratulatory message can be surprisingly uplifting. Consider a digital "victory wall" for sharing achievements and stories of overcoming self-doubt. The aim isn't perfection —it's progress and resilience.

Rotating roles and exchanging resources—articles, podcasts, tools— strengthens your squad. Over time, casual check-ins may grow into genuine friendships or professional collaborations. Your support squad will likely become a favorite part of your goal-setting journey; nothing tops knowing people have your back during tough times and share in your successes.

Sample Agenda Template: Squad Check-In

- Welcome & mood check (1-2 minutes each)
- Wins: Share a recent success
- Challenges: Name your current obstacle
- Brainstorm/spotlight: The Group intensely focuses on one member's dilemma
- Next steps: Everyone commits to one action
- Celebration: End with a cheer or digital high-five

Stay flexible—add humor if things get heavy, and keep it brief if energy is low. Your support squad is about more than just account-ability—building true resilience with people who genuinely understand.

SELF-COMPASSION FOR GOAL-GETTERS—BOUNCING BACK WITHOUT BEATING YOURSELF UP

Facing setbacks, it's common to turn inward with harsh self-criticism —replaying regrets, magnifying mistakes, and letting an inner critic override all sense of progress. Yet research, notably from Dr. Kristin Neff and colleagues, shows that self-compassion is anything but a feel-good cliché. Treating yourself kindly after disappointment is a proven driver of motivation, resilience, and long-term performance. Far from promoting complacency, self-compassion helps people learn from failures, recover faster, and pursue challenging goals with renewed commitment. In short, grit with warmth outperforms perpetual self-flagellation.

How do you practice self-compassion in the face of setbacks? Start with a "self-kindness script." When you miss a goal or hit a wall, pause and consider how a supportive friend would respond—one who listens and encourages without judgment. Write a brief note from their viewpoint: "It's okay to struggle sometimes. You're juggling a lot and learning as you go. Setbacks are normal." Say it out loud if possi-ble; if it feels uncomfortable, that's a sign you probably need it.

Compassionate journaling is another effective tool. Spend a few minutes writing a letter to yourself as you would to a loved one, using gentle and supportive language: "I know you tried hard—it's normal to feel frustrated, but this moment doesn't define you." Over time, this helps your brain respond to failure calmly instead of shame, making it easier to move past disappointment and try again.

Mantras can help reset your mindset in the moment. If you notice harsh self-talk, interrupt it with truths like, "I am learning, and this is part of growth." It may initially feel strange, but repetition gradually changes your internal narrative.

Understanding the boundary between healthy self-reflection and toxic self-criticism is key. Constructive self-reflection asks, "What worked? Where did I get stuck? What can I change next time?" It focuses on actions, not identity, and feels solution-oriented, even if uncomfortable. In contrast, self-criticism jumps to character attacks: "I always fail," "I'll never get it right." The former builds insight, while the latter erodes motivation.

Self-Reflection vs. Self-Criticism Table

Self-Reflection Example Self-Criticism Example: "That deadline was tight—next time, I'll start earlier." "I'm such a procrastinator." "Missing two workouts signals I need to tweak my schedule." "I have no discipline." "What distracted me this week?" "I can't keep anything together." "I'm glad I tried, even if it wasn't perfect." "I shouldn't have even tried."

Notice: reflection stays action- and pattern-focused and never attacks your worth. Criticism uses harsh absolutes ("always," "never," "can't") and targets your character.

Rebounding quickly from setbacks means creating a ritual that signals self-care and progress, without guilt. Maybe that looks like a mindful walk without ruminating, listening to a mood-boosting song, and jotting down a lesson learned. Add a tangible act of self-care—good food, rest, or reaching out to a friend. Connecting with yourself compassionately clears shame and lets you review your next steps with a renewed mind.

For extra structure, note three things: one that went wrong (without blame), one that you did right (however small), and one that you'll try next. This simple reflection wipes away shame and makes progress feel possible again.

The big picture: seeking kindness isn't a weakness—it's intelligent fuel for persistence. Self-compassion isn't about excusing yourself or lowering standards; it's about creating the psychological safety to keep striving. So next time you stumble—as everyone does—remember proper recovery begins with treating yourself as a person worth supporting.

Ultimately, resilience is about bouncing back, not beating yourself up. Self-compassion is essential, whether you're recovering from small slips or major setbacks. Next, we'll look at how to sustain your wins long after the initial spark of success fades.

How you inspire others to be the best version of themselves. That is true success.

— KOBE BRYANT

VICTORY, EVOLUTION, AND LEGACY—SUSTAINING SUCCESS AND INSPIRING OTHERS

THE 30-DAY GOAL SPRINT CHALLENGE— SUPERCHARGING MOMENTUM

Imagine being at the starting line of a race: half-prepared, nervous, and eager but doubtful. Now, imagine being handed a turbo-charged skateboard with the encouragement to stay focused for just 30 days. The 30-Day Goal Sprint Challenge is that burst of focused action—a sharp, energized interval that pushes you further in one month than months of slow, scattered effort. Where marathons call for pacing and often cause fatigue before real progress, the sprint model is about harnessing intense energy and attention for a clearly defined, short-term target. It's about progress you can see and feel quickly, turning effort into instant momentum.

The difference between a marathon and a sprint is key: Marathons are for huge endeavors where endurance is critical, but their distant finish lines can sap your energy. A sprint, by contrast, means thirty days of laser focus on just one goal—a "high-intensity" burst in your personal growth routine. The real win is quick results and momentum that can spill into your broader ambitions.

How do you pick a good sprint goal? Don't shoot for the moon—keep sprint goals micro-sized yet mighty. Think "Send twenty job applications," "Finish a short creative project," or "Stick to a new morning routine"—anything achievable in 30 days with meaningful impact. The secret is specificity and actionability. Ask: "What's one thing I could make real progress on in 30 days that would make my life or goals easier or set me up for bigger success?" Brainstorm a list and narrow it down based on realistic effort and the biggest payoff.

With your micro-goal set, break it into daily actions—thirty micro-steps, one for each day. These should be so simple that you can do them even on a tough day. For instance, writing 9,000 words is just 300 per day. Networking? One new message a day. Decluttering? One shelf or drawer—done. Bite-sized wins keep motivation high and achievement visible.

Track your actions using a simple 30-day calendar—on paper, in a spreadsheet, or through an app. Fill each day's box with your micro-action and leave space for a celebration sticker or emoji once you complete it. These visible streaks trigger your brain's reward system, making you want to keep the habit alive (University of Minnesota Extension, n.d.).

When motivation lags in the middle of your sprint, scheduled mini celebrations can drive you forward. Don't wait for Day 30 to celebrate. Reward yourself every five or seven days: enjoy a favorite treat, go for an extra-long walk with good music, or share your streak for virtual high-fives. Celebrating even small steps keeps dopamine flowing and engagement up (University of Minnesota Extension, n.d.).

No plan—no matter how well designed—survives reality unscathed. Weekly checkpoints are essential. Every seven days, pause and reflect: What's going well? What's challenging? What needs adjusting? If your daily task feels overwhelming or tedious, halve it or swap in something new but aligned with your goal. Flexibility shows wisdom, not failure (Rotman School of Management Insights Hub, 2024). Progress often accelerates because you modify and adapt rather than persist with a failing plan.

For instance, if your original goal was reading 20 pages a night and you keep falling asleep, switch to audiobooks during your commute or lunch. If morning runs aren't sticking, shift to evenings. Revise your calendar to match your reality.

A sample week-by-week networking sprint could look like:

- **Week 1:** Research leads and send your first message.
- **Week 2:** Keep messaging daily; track responses.
- **Week 3:** Follow up with interested parties; set up one virtual coffee.
- **Week 4:** Reflect; identify the most meaningful connections. Plan what's next.

You can use the sprint model for any goal, from fitness to decluttering to creative projects.

Don't underestimate the impact of the community on achieving your sprint. While you might muscle through 30 days solo, public commitment and group support multiply your accountability (Lisa Hoashi, n.d.). Join or create a "Goal Sprint" group online or chat with friends. A hashtag like #VictorySprint2025 can give your challenge extra fanfare.

Group participation isn't just about posting wins. Share struggles, obstacles, or simply a celebratory GIF. Normalizing effort—ups and downs—makes sticking with it easier. Daily or weekly check-ins strengthen positive peer pressure and mutual encouragement.

Interactive Element: Your Printable 30-Day Sprint Planner

To launch your sprint, use a straightforward planner:

1. **Pick Your Micro-Goal:** Write it at the top ("Walk 6,000 steps daily," "Write one poem every day," "Declutter one area each evening").
2. **Daily Actions:** Fill each day's box (e.g., "Text accountability buddy," "Send LinkedIn invite," "Sort a folder").
3. **Mini-Rewards:** Mark every 5th or 7th day for a reward ("Treat: coffee break!" "Dance party!" "Share progress!").
4. **Weekly Reflections:** On days 7, 14, 21, and 28, answer:
   ○ What went well this week?
   ○ What needed adjustment?
   ○ Am I getting results?
   ○ What am I proud of?
5. **Adapt As Needed:** If an action feels too hard or dull, scale it back or swap it for something engaging.
6. **Share Progress:** Daily or weekly, post in your group or update an accountability partner.

Customize the planner—sketch it on blank paper, color-code it in a spreadsheet, or try a habit tracker app (ClickUp, 2025).

The point isn't perfect execution but consistent daily action around what's meaningful to you. Extraordinary outcomes come from stringing together many small, ordinary efforts.

You may surprise yourself after 30 days—completing that long-stalled draft, turning exercise from a chore to a favorite ritual, or setting habits that last. If doubts creep in ("Is this working?"), Use those weekly reflection points to recalibrate, not just check off boxes. Adaptation is the real engine of lasting progress.

A sprint is less about perfection and more about discovery—learning what happens when you devote thirty days of honest effort to one priority and let that momentum propel you forward.

PASSING THE TORCH—BECOMING AN INSPIRATION AND ACCOUNTABILITY PARTNER

Witnessing someone else accomplish what seemed impossible can be transformative. When I saw a friend post about completing her first 5K, my excuses for not exercising lost their power. That's the ripple effect: sharing honest progress sparks belief and action, not just in us but in others—friends, teammates, even strangers scrolling through social media. Sharing your story, with all its messiness and milestones, becomes contagious motivation. Speaking your journey aloud —failures, lessons, and victories—cements your growth. The act itself becomes accountability, making progress more real than keeping quiet.

Psychological research shows that telling your story increases empathy and motivation for the teller and the listener. Sharing struggles and breakthroughs helps others feel less alone and reinforces your own sense of growth. You don't need to wait for some "finish line" to start sharing; honesty about imperfect starts or rough patches is often more encouraging than a string of polished achievements. If opening about failure feels awkward, remember that your honesty could be the lifeline someone else needs.

Now, let's talk about the accountability partner or mentor role. Don't picture a formal, intimidating setup; adequate support is casual and enjoyable. The best accountability partners are goal buddies: part cheerleader, sounding board, and reality check. You don't need to boss anyone or dispense constant advice. Instead, focus on listening, reflecting, and supporting. No judgment is the key.

Set up a regular check-in, ideally for about 15-30 minutes weekly. Start by asking what your buddy has planned since the last time and how it went. Celebrate successes, and if things fall short, calmly discuss barriers and brainstorm what might help next. Your job is to echo what you hear ("So, work got wild?") more than handing out solutions unless specifically asked. People often find their own answers when someone listens attentively.

For deeper support, try co-working: meet up, state your goals ("I'll write for 30 minutes," "I'll reply to three emails," etc.), work together quietly, and debrief. These shared sessions boost motivation and turn mundane tasks into something communal, even fun, especially if you celebrate afterward with a small treat or a meme.

Aim for genuine, relatable updates when sharing your story with others, on social media or privately. Avoid bragging or humblebragging; people value honest reflection over perfection. A simple template is:

- **Win:** [what you achieved]
- **Challenge:** [what was hard]
- **Lesson:** [an insight that helps others]
- Example: "Win: Wrote every morning but Tuesday! Challenge: My dog ate my planner. Lesson: Even tiny wins count, and sometimes backup plans matter."

Alternatively, try a roundtable with friends or coworkers: share one goal milestone, challenge, tip, or lesson. Keep it relaxed (snacks, coffee) and focus on humor and honesty rather than formal presentations.

To keep it real, avoid preaching. Instead of dispensing advice—unless asked—offer your experience as just one possible way forward: "This helped me when I was stuck—it might give you an idea." This respects everyone's journey and doesn't add unnecessary pressure.

Mentorship is most potent when it's collaborative. You don't need all the answers; being a partner sometimes means asking, "What do you want to try next?" or "How can I support you this week?" Holding space for someone to brainstorm is sometimes more helpful than giving advice.

You can also encourage group accountability. Propose goal buddy systems at work or in a student club, where people check in weekly or rotate partners for new perspectives. Or create a group chat for daily intentions and midweek mini wins. These small communities build positive peer support and normalize progress.

To expand your impact, seek leadership opportunities: start a mastermind group, host monthly meetups for project sharing and honest feedback, or volunteer to speak at local events or webinars about your personal experience with goals and habits. No expertise is required—just candor about what worked (and didn't). Real stories far more inspire people than by advice from supposed experts.

If you need structure when sharing or leading, try these templates:

Social Media Reflection Template:

- Win: [What did I accomplish?]
- Challenge: [What was tough?]
- Lesson: [What did I learn?]
- Next step: [What's next?]
- Example: "Win: Asked my boss for feedback (scary, but worth it!). Challenge: Overthinking emails. Lesson: Most worries are noise—I survived! Next: Try batching email replies."

Goal Roundtable Script:

- "Let's each share a recent win, a challenge we hit, and one insight that surprised us."
- "What helped you keep going when motivation dropped?"
- "Anyone discover a helpful trick or tool this week?"

Group Accountability Message:

- "Checking in! My goal this week was [X], hit trouble with [Y], learned [Z]. Still going—any tips?"

Passing the torch doesn't require expertise or formality—only the willingness to openly support and grow together. The ripple effect is real: every shared story makes it easier for someone else to try.

Setting up these systems is simple. Find a cadence (weekly calls, monthly roundtables, ongoing chat) and agree on ground rules (judgment-free, equal speaking time, advice only when asked, celebration of all progress, setbacks are just data).

As you step up to support others, you'll find that cheering for their progress boosts your motivation, too. Seeing others wrestle with setbacks normalizes your own, and group brainstorming sparks new ideas for everyone.

Teaching, mentoring, or even simply supporting is an incredible way to deepen one's own learning and resilience. Your encouragement returns to you; each story you share builds your confidence, and every supportive act strengthens your growth.

So, whether you're nudging a friend out of a rut, organizing a workplace roundtable, or posting honest updates online that make someone feel less alone—know that your influence goes further than you realize. The torch shines brighter with every handoff; your willingness to support and share keeps the light moving forward.

CREATING YOUR LASTING LEGACY—FROM PERSONAL VICTORY TO COLLECTIVE IMPACT

There comes a point when the glow of personal achievement stretches beyond your boundaries. You've hit some significant milestones and weathered storms, and now a new question floats up: What does all this progress mean for someone besides you? Take a minute and think—how do your wins, pivots, and hard-earned lessons ripple outward? Maybe your kids or siblings believe they can go after something bigger. Perhaps your team at work gets bolder with their ideas, or a friend texts you, "Because you did it, I might try too." The truth is that every personal breakthrough can potentially change the atmosphere for those around you. One person's courage often gives permission for others to step forward. So, your growth isn't just about what you get—it's about what you make possible for your family, coworkers, and circle of influence.

I love this prompt: "How does your success change what's possible for your family, team, or community?" Answering it can initially feel awkward—almost like bragging—but it's not about ego. It's about recognizing that you open a new door for others whenever you overcome fear or finish something meaningful. Think of it as clearing a walking trail through thick woods; the path you carve makes it easier for someone else to follow, maybe even run. For parents, that might look like modeling resilience or work ethic. For team leaders, it could be setting new standards for collaboration or innovation. Even in friend groups, your willingness to try (and fail and try again) can make risk-taking feel safer for everyone.

Now, let's get practical about making this impact stick. Growth can be fleeting if you don't document what worked, what didn't, and the real "aha" moments. This doesn't mean writing a memoir (unless you want to!), but it does mean capturing the process in some form, so it's not lost to time or busy schedules. One powerful way is to create your own "legacy playbook." This is simply a digital or physical collection of the routines, mindsets, scripts, and oddball tricks that helped you move forward. You could jot down your favorite daily prompts or sketch your go-to problem-solving flowchart. You might record video reflections on days when things clicked (or fell apart spectacularly). Over time, this becomes a toolkit for yourself and anyone you mentor or support during tough patches.

You don't need fancy software or a graphic designer. Open a blank document and start with headings like: "What I Do When I'm Stuck," "My Best Motivation Rituals," "Lessons Learned from Big Mess-Ups," and "Small Wins That Built Momentum." If you're more visual or talkative, use your phone's camera and do short video diaries. These don't have to go public; sharing them with one person who needs a boost— or with your future self—can make a difference. You could even turn these artifacts into blog posts or an email series for mentees or colleagues who ask, "How did you do it?" The key is to codify what's unique about your approach so it can be adapted and passed on.

Moving from personal notes to broader impact can take many forms, but one of the most powerful is "institutionalizing" what you've learned. It sounds fancy, but it just embeds your approach into the systems or groups where you spend time. If you're part of a team or club that struggles with goal follow-through, design a workshop based on your experience—walk them through what worked for you, complete with exercises and real stories (bonus points if they're embarrassing). If your workplace is open to new ideas, suggest a training session on habit-building or resilience. These don't have to be TED-level productions; sometimes the simplest formats land best—a lunch-and-learn, a shared Google Doc of checklists and prompts, or even an informal roundtable where people swap tips on getting unstuck.

For those who want to go even further—maybe you feel called to create a bigger legacy—think about starting something lasting that lines up with your values. Start a scholarship for students pursuing goals that matter to you, set up a fund for creative projects in your neighborhood, or launch a club that gives people regular space to work on meaningful personal targets. The project doesn't have to be massive; even small initiatives can have outsized effects when they're consistent and accurate to your story. The point is to build something that keeps paying forward your lessons long after the initial spark.

If you're leading teams at work or involved in organizations, consider how your systems or rituals could become part of how things are done. Please build regular reflection time into meetings. Create shared "Wins Walls" in the break room? Add personal goal check-ins to onboarding or training programs? Little tweaks like these can shift culture over time, making growth and experimentation routine instead of rare exceptions.

Of course, no legacy worth building stays frozen in time. Circumstances change, and so do we. That's why ongoing evolution is so important. The goals that mattered most to you five years ago might be different today—and that's normal and healthy. Try setting up an annual "legacy review to keep your impact relevant and alive." Block off an hour once a year (maybe on your birthday or at year's end) and ask yourself: What impact did I have this year? Which lessons still feel true? What new ambitions am I ready to chase? This isn't just reflection; it's also about updating your vision statement and letting your circle know what's next on your radar.

Sharing these updates—whether in a group email, a quick team huddle, or a family dinner—reminds everyone that growth never stops at one finish line. Please invite others to share their new ambitions, too; this turns legacy into a living conversation rather than something carved in stone.

Reflection Exercise: Your Legacy Blueprint

Take ten minutes right now. Jot down responses to these prompts:

- In what ways does my progress open doors for others?
- What key routines or lessons would I want someone else to use?
- How could I share these in my family, workplace, or community?
- What action could I take this year to institutionalize my approach?
- When will I schedule my first legacy review?

Don't overthink it—write honestly and see what surfaces.

Legacy isn't about having buildings named after you or trending on social media for an hour. It's about leaving behind habits, mindsets, and choices that outlast any win. It's passing along courage in tangible ways—through stories told at dinner tables, systems built into teams, rituals handed down at meetings or meetups, and small acts of encouragement that echo through generations.

As we wrap up this chapter, remember: Your success isn't just a trophy on a mental shelf—it's a toolkit for others and an invitation to keep building something bigger than yourself. Growth doesn't end; it multiplies. Your legacy starts now—with every new step you take and every lesson you choose to share.

And here's the beauty: every bit of progress adds another brick to the path for those who will walk it after you. Your growth doesn't just lift you—it lifts everyone who sees that progress is possible. Keep building forward. There's always another chapter ahead.

CONCLUSION

Look at you—still here at the end of this book, curious and hungry for growth. I hope you brought snacks because this is the victory lap. And you deserve to savor it.

Let's rewind for a second. Remember where we started? Maybe you picked up this book with a vague sense of "I should get it together." Maybe your list of unfinished goals was longer than your streaming queue. Perhaps you just wanted to figure out why you keep buying planners, only to abandon them by February (guilty as charged, by the way).

But look at the ground you've covered. You didn't just read; you rolled up your sleeves and did the work. You took your scattered hopes and gave them shape. You learned to sort real dreams from other people's "shoulds." You must be honest about what motivates you, what slows you down, and how to build systems that don't collapse when life throws you a curveball (because it will, and probably when you're wearing your good shirt).

Unstuck's journey was never about becoming a productivity robot. It was about becoming more you. You've moved through ten significant phases: clarifying your vision, getting specific about what matters, building a mindset that helps you bounce back, and focusing on the goals that light you up. You mapped out action steps, broke big dreams into bite-sized wins, and made space for progress even when your calendar looked like a game of Tetris.

We tackled the real-life stuff: how to keep moving when motivation fizzles, how to celebrate small wins, how to track progress without turning into a spreadsheet zombie, and how to recover when you faceplant (because nobody is immune). We dug into the messy middle —burnout, setbacks, pivots—because that's where most people quit. But not you. You've built a toolkit for resilience, reflection, and realignment.

If you take away nothing else, remember this: meaningful change doesn't come from perfect plans or color-coded calendars. It comes from clarity—knowing what you want and why. It comes from practical action—showing up, even on the days you'd rather not. And it comes from reflection—pausing to notice, "Hey, I'm further along than I thought." You don't have to do it all at once. You must do the next right thing.

Here's the best part: no one "right" way exists. Your version of victory doesn't have to look like anyone else's. The tools in this book are here for you to tweak, remix, and toss out as needed. Maybe you thrive with sticky notes on your mirror. Perhaps you need a digital tracker, a group chat, or a playlist that makes you feel like the main character in your movie. Personalize everything. Make it yours. Your goals, your pace, your flavor of weirdness—own it.

Before you stuff this book on a shelf and return to doomscrolling, take a second to celebrate. Yes, you. You showed up for yourself. Maybe you haven't crossed every finish line yet, but you've moved forward. And that's a win. That's a bunch of wins stacked together like pancakes. (And you know how I feel about pancakes.)

You've also learned that setbacks aren't the end of the story. They're just plot twists. You can bounce back stronger every time with your new recovery tools, mindset shifts, and support systems. You're not just a goal-setter now—you're a goal-getter, a pivot-master, a come-back artist.

So, here's your next challenge: don't just think about what you've learned—do something with it. Pick one step. Maybe it's filling out the reflection prompt at the end of this chapter. Perhaps it's jumping into the online community (yes, you're invited—no secret handshake required). Maybe it's starting the 30-Day Goal Sprint and seeing how much can change in a month. Action turns knowledge into momentum. Don't wait for "someday." Start now, even if your only tool is a napkin and a pencil stub.

And don't keep this journey to yourself. Share your story. Be the person who cheers others on, admits when it gets tough, and celebrates every tiny victory. Sign up as an accountability buddy or start your own "Wins Wall" at work or school. Tell your story with all its honest, messy, glorious details. When you shine a light, you help others see what's possible.

You're not in this alone. I'm still cheering you on, and so is everyone who's ever tried, failed, and tried again. Stay connected—find resources, updates, and a community of fellow dreamers and doers. Reach out, swap ideas, trade memes, or say, "Hey, I'm still in the game."

Here's what I hope you remember as you step into your next chapter: Your victories matter. Your setbacks don't define you. Your willingness to keep moving, to adapt, to laugh at yourself, and to keep showing up—that's what turns vision into victory. That's how you leave a mark, not just for yourself but for everyone who gets a little braver because they saw you try.

So, take a bow. Then, take your next step. The finish line isn't the end —it's just another starting line waiting for you to cross again and again. Make your vision real. I'll be rooting for you every step of the way.

WE'D LOVE TO HEAR FROM YOU!

Thank you for taking the time to read this book. Your support means more than you know, and I truly hope the insights, strategies, and reflections shared throughout these pages have made a meaningful impact on your journey.

If this book has inspired you, challenged your thinking, or helped you take a step forward, I would be incredibly grateful if you would take a moment to leave a review.

Why Your Review Matters

Your feedback:

- Helps other readers discover this book
- Provides valuable insights for future editions and content
- Encourages continued work in creating resources that make a difference

How to Leave a Review

You can leave a review on:

- Amazon
- Barnes & Noble
- Goodreads
- Or wherever you purchased this book

A Few Questions to Guide Your Review

If you're not sure where to start, consider sharing:

- What was your biggest takeaway from the book?
- How has this book impacted your thinking or actions?

- Who would you recommend this book to and why?

Stay Connected

I would love to hear more about your journey and how you're applying what you've learned. Feel free to connect, share your story, and continue growing. Check us out on www.chooselegacy.net or follow our social media pages.

Thank you again for your support—it truly makes a difference.

With gratitude,

Dr. Valarie Henry

REFERENCES

- Ackerman, C. E. (2025, January 15). *25 self-reflection questions: Why introspection is important.* PositivePsychology.com. https://positivepsychology.com/intro spection-self-reflection/
- Asana. (2025). *10 limiting beliefs and how to overcome them.* https://asana.com/ resources/limiting-beliefs
- Asana. (2025). *The Eisenhower Matrix: How to prioritize your to-do list.* https:// asana.com/resources/eisenhower-matrix
- Association for Psychological Science. (2015, November 10). *Why Monday is the best day for setting new goals.* https://www.psychologicalscience.org/news/ minds-business/why-monday-is-the-best-day-for-setting-new-goals.html
- Atypical Finance. (2024). *4 steps to reverse engineer your goals and make them easier to reach.* https://www.atypicalfinance.com/4-steps-reverse-engineer-goals-make-easier-reach/
- Business News Daily. (2024, May 17). *Best goal-tracking tools.* https://www. businessnewsdaily.com/10495-track-goals-tools.html
- Calm. (2023). *How to set personal goals and 8 ways to achieve them.* Calm. https:// www.calm.com/blog/personal-goals
- ClickUp. (2025, June 9). *10 best goal tracking apps for 2025 (free & paid).* https:// clickup.com/blog/goal-tracking-apps/
- Clear, J. (n.d.). *How to build new habits by taking advantage of old ones.* https:// jamesclear.com/habit-stacking
- Farnam Street. (2025). *Carol Dweck: A summary of growth and fixed mindsets.* https://fs.blog/carol-dweck-mindset/
- Forbes Business Council. (2023, May 18). *The power of mastermind groups: Unlocking success for business owners.* Forbes. https://www.forbes.com/coun cils/forbesbusinesscouncil/2023/05/18/the-power-of-curated-mastermind-groups-unlocking-success-for-business-owners/
- Forbes Coaches Council. (2021, May 6). *Four brain science habits to help neutralize negative self-talk.* Forbes. https://www.forbes.com/councils/ forbescoachescouncil/2021/05/06/four-brain-science-habits-to-help-neutral ize-negative-self-talk/
- Frates, N. (2025). *Visualization and goal achievement: Science and best practices.* https://www.nickfrates.com/blog/visualization-and-goal-achievement-sci ence-psychology-and-best-practices
- Gallup (2025). CliftonStrengths. https://www.gallup.com/cliftonstrengths/ en/254033/strengthsfinder.aspx
- Goldstein, S. (n.d.). *Grief: The path to letting go of expectations in ourselves and our relationships.* Goldstein Therapy. http://goldsteintherapy.com/grief-the-path-to-letting-go-of-expectations-in-ourselves-and-our-relationships/

- Hoashi, L. (n.d.). *How to set up an accountability partnership*. https://www.lisa hoashi.com/blog/accountability-partner
- Huang, Szu-chi & Jin, Liyin & Zhang, Ying. (2017). Step by Step: Sub-Goals as a Source of Motivation. Organizational Behavior and Human Decision Processes. 141. 10.1016/j.obhdp.2017.05.001.
- LDH World. (n.d.). *The 30-day life sprint: A practical plan*. https://www.ldhworld.com/ldh-world/the-30-day-life-sprint-a-practical-plan#:~:text=Instead%20of%20vague%20goals%2C%20sets,in%20half%20the%20usual%20time.
- Lefebvre, M., Gocine, A., Clough, B., & Grossman, P. (2020). *Self-compassion and resilience at work: A practice-oriented approach*. https://self-compassion.org/wp-content/uploads/2021/11/Lefebvre-et-al.-2020-Self-Compassion-and-Resilience-at-Work-A-Practice.pdf
- Life Intelligence. (2024, April 2). *The rhythm of productivity: How to determine your peak productive hours*. https://cms.lifeintelligencegroup.com/blog/the-rhythm-of-productivity-how-to-determine-your-peak-productive-hours
- Marie, M. (n.d.). *How to stay focused on your goals when life gets busy*. https://www.muriellemarie.com/blog/how-to-stay-focused-on-your-goals-when-life-gets-busy
- Norton, J. (2025, February 2). *Redefining success: Create new metrics for a meaningful life*. Psychology Today. https://www.psychologytoday.com/us/blog/empower-your-mind/202502/redefining-success-create-new-metrics-for-a-meaningful-life
- Notion. (2025). *Top 10 free weekly action plan templates*. https://www.notion.com/templates/collections/top-10-free-weekly-action-plan-templates-in-notion
- Quire. (2023, December 12). *6 proven steps for a recovery plan after a career setback*. https://quire.io/blog/p/career-recovery.html
- Rachitsky, L. (2024). *My favorite decision making frameworks*. Lenny's Newsletter. https://www.lennysnewsletter.com/p/my-favorite-decision-making-frameworks
- Reyes, N. L. (2020, January 3). *How to say no: 12 phrases & scripts that won't make the sky fall down*. https://baggagereclaim.co.uk/how-to-say-no-12-phrases-scripts-that-wont-make-the-sky-fall-down/
- Rotman School of Management. (2024, January). *The art of the goal pivot: When and how to change direction*. https://www-2.rotman.utoronto.ca/insightshub/leadership-career-development/pivot-your-goals
- Seattle Neurocounseling. (n.d.). *Embracing failure: Harnessing the power of failing forward*. https://seattleneurocounseling.com/blog-1/failingforward
- SHRM Executive Network. (2023, July 5). *A guide to understanding & preventing burnout as an executive*. https://www.shrm.org/executive-network/insights/guide-to-understanding-preventing-burnout-executive
- Sinek, S. (2017, September 5). *Find your WHY book | Go beyond reading*. Simon Sinek. https://simonsinek.com/books/find-your-why/

- Success Alliance. (n.d.). *Mastermind groups versus accountability groups.* https://www.thesuccessalliance.com/blog/mastermind-groups-versus-accountability-groups/
- The Psychology Group. (n.d.). *What is getting in the way of you achieving your goals?* https://thepsychologygroup.com/what-to-do-about-f-e-a-r/
- Todoist. (n.d.). *The complete guide to deep work.* https://www.todoist.com/inspiration/deep-work
- Todoist. (n.d.). *Time blocking — Your complete guide to more focused work.* https://www.todoist.com/productivity-methods/time-blocking
- Thrive Global. (2017, August 21). *Build your playbook for life.* https://medium.com/thrive-global/build-your-playbook-for-life-1b7ca86df4e3
- Travers, M. (2024, March 29). *A psychologist explains the power of 'vision boarding' for success.* Forbes. https://www.forbes.com/sites/traversmark/2024/03/29/a-psychologist-explains-the-power-of-vision-boarding-for-success/
- University of Minnesota Extension. (n.d.). *Celebrate the small stuff | Positive psychology.* https://extension.umn.edu/two-you-video-series/celebrate-small-stuff
- UserGuiding. (n.d.). *How to create a goal tracking system that works.* https://userguiding.com/blog/goal-tracking-system
- Visionary Currents. (2024, October 19). *How to reframe failure as feedback: The pathway to continuous improvement.* https://medium.com/visionary-currents/how-to-reframe-failure-as-feedback-the-pathway-to-continuous-improvement-fa27068f600a
- Wang, X., Wong, K., & Yuen, K. S. L. (2022). A potential mechanism linking problematic social media use and suicide risk. *Frontiers in Public Health, 10,* 929524. https://pmc.ncbi.nlm.nih.gov/articles/PMC9295248/

www.ingramcontent.com/pod-product-compliance
Lightning Source LLC
Chambersburg PA
CBHW071257130626
46556CB00003B/1352